SUPERCARRIERS

NAVAL AVIATION IN ACTION

SUPERCARRIERS

NAVAL AVIATION IN ACTION

TONY HOLMES

OSPREY
AVIATION

First published in Great Britain in 2000 by Osprey Publishing
Elms Court, Chapel Way, Botley, Oxford, OX2- 9LP, UK
E-mail: info@ospreypublishing.com

ISBN 1 84176 026 9

Written and edited by Tony Holmes
Page design by TT Designs, T & B Truscott
Origination by Valhaven, Isleworth, UK
Printed through Bookbuilders, Hong Kong

00 01 02 03 04   10 9 8 7 6 5 4 3 2 1

Acknowledgements

During my 14 years of covering naval aviation, the welcome that I have received on each and every ship that I have visited has been memorable. Although only aboard for 72 hours at most, I have always been made to feel as if I was a fully-fledged member of the crew.

Countless individuals have helped with the compilation of this book, and although I cannot name them all because of the lack of space (and, in some cases, due to security restrictions imposed by the US Navy), the following men and women have proven invaluable in seeing the project through to fruition.

US Navy

Vice Admiral Charles W 'Willy' Moore, Commander, Fifth Fleet; Rear Admiral Timothy J Keating, Commander, Carrier Group Five; Capt Rick McHarg, Commander, Carrier Air Wing Five; Cdr J D Gradeck, Commander, Fifth Fleet PAO; Cdr Dave Petri, Safety Officer CVN 70; Cdr Ron Sandoval, Commander, HS-6; Cdr Tom Twomey; Lt Cdr Gary Smilowitz, CINCUSNAVEUR; Lt(jg) Charlie Brown and Chief Brian O'Rourke, PAO Naval Air Forces Pacific; Lt Cdr Scott Harrison, PAO CVN 72; Lt Dave Waterman, PAO CVN 70; Lt Mark Boyd, PAO CV 63; Lts Brenda Malone and Daren Pelkie, Fifth Fleet PAOs; Lt 'Zeno' Rausa, VFA-94 and VFA-122; Lt(jg) Peter Fey, VAQ-135; the crew of 'Knight 616', Lts Mike Steffen and Jack McLaughlin, AW2 Luis Borges and AW3 Dennis Josse; the crew of 'Indian 614', Lts Tamara Karowski and Billy Fraser, and AWC Mark Weaver; the crew of 'Lightning 617', Lt Cdrs Scott Blackwood and Ron Ravelo, AW1 Elmer DePalma and AW3 Mike Iwicki; Capt (ret) 'Zip' Rausa; Cdr (ret) Peter Mersky

Civilians

Ian Glanville of British Airways; Graham Armitage of Sigma UK; Richard Suidak of ANA Squadron 55; David Peters; Eve Taylor

Photographic Information

All the photographs featured in *Supercarriers* were taken using either Nikon F4 or N90S camera bodies, fitted with Nikkor or Sigma AF lenses ranging in size from 24 mm through to 400 mm. The latter were fitted with Hoya UV or Skylight 1B filters for optical protection purposes only. The film exposed was exclusively Fujichrome Velvia 50 ASA or Provia 100 ASA professional stock

Editor's note

The Editor would be pleased to receive comments on the editorial content of this book. Please write to Tony Holmes at 10 Prospect Road, Sevenoaks, Kent, TN13 3UA, Great Britain, or by e-mail at: tony.holmes@osprey-jets.freeserve.co.uk

FRONT COVER The 'Tip of the Spear'. USS *Carl Vinson* (CVN 70) cuts through the calm waters of the northern Persian Gulf during the carrier's record 89-day stint 'on the line' enforcing the no-fly zone over southern Iraq during its *WestPac '98/99* deployment

TITLE PAGE Having completed yet another Operation *Southern Watch* (OSW) patrol, VF-213's 'Blacklion 102' (BuNo 164602) and '111' (BuNo 161159) are pushed back into traditional fighter 'territory' on the fantail of CVN 70. The Tomcat in the foreground carries a Lockheed Martin AN/AAQ-14 LANTIRN (Low Altitude Navigation and Targeting Infra-Red for Night) pod on Station 8B, above which is a storeless LAU-7 missile launcher rail, incorporating a CelsiusTech BOL chaff dispenser within its structure. The LANTIRN pod made its operational debut over Bosnia in 1996, and has drastically improved the F-14's capabilities as a bomber. I was left in no doubt of this fact by a RIO from VF-213;

'The dual cockpit of the Tomcat is a real asset for the missions that we are performing on OSW, particularly when we are flying a jet equipped with a LANTIRN pod. We have an unfair advantage with this system because we have two guys to split the workload, using better displays. The Hornet pilots, by contrast, really have their work cut out for them, as they have to find the target using a display that is not as clear as ours, *and* fly the jet at the same time. In the Tomcat, the pilot gets on with flying the mission, whilst the RIO concentrates exclusively on the targeting'.

BuNo 164602 was the third from last F-14 built by Grumman, being issued to VF-124 on 1 May 1992. It then moved to VF-2, before being reassigned to VF-213 in late 1997

TITLE VERSO PAGE Bathed in warm evening light, 'Beefeater 303' (BuNo 164018) of VFA-22 'Redcocks' sits patiently on CVN 70's waist cat four in preparation for launching on an OSW mission during CVW-11's 1998-99 *WestPac*. On the port 'shoulder' station can be seen an AAS-38B NITE (Navigational Infra-red Targeting Equipment) Hawk FLIR-LTD/R (Forward-Looking Infra-Red Laser Target Designator/Ranger) pod, this device being an almost permanent fixture on all Hornets flying operationally in the Persian Gulf

CONTENTS PAGE Obscured by steam rising from CVN 70's waist cat three, green-shirted catapult crewmen set themselves for the launch of a heavily-loaded F-14D from waist four. Behind them, a second Tomcat is only minutes away from taking its cat stroke. The board held by the figure to the left is used to instruct the pilot on the estimated weight of his/her aircraft, and the latter individual has to visually confirm this with the catapult crew prior to the aircraft being cleared for launching. The weight is used to calculate the amount of pressure that is required to successfully launch the aircraft – and judging by the sheer bulk of the Tomcat out of shot, a good head of steam was needed to get if off the deck

For a catalogue of all books published by Osprey Military and Aviation please write to:

Osprey Direct UK, PO Box 140, Wellingborough, Northants NN8 4ZA, United Kingdom • Email:info@ospreydirect.co.uk

Osprey Direct USA, PO Box 130, Sterling Heights, MI 48311-0130, USA • Email:info@ospreydirectusa.com

OR VISIT US AT
www.ospreypublishing.com

CONTENTS

SUPERCARRIERS - A PERSONAL INTRODUCTION

The publication of this book marks the first occasion that I have had an all-new photographic volume on carrier aviation produced by Osprey Aviation Publishing since the release of *World Supercarriers* in the summer of 1988. In the intervening 12 years, I have been fortunate enough to photo-edit material from some of the world's best aviation photographers – individuals of the calibre of George Hall, Ian Black, John Dibbs and Michael O'Leary, to name but four.

These individuals, and numerous others from across the globe, contributed to a list of books known as the Osprey Colour Series (and its various offshoots such as the Superbase series). At the leading edge of illustrated aviation publishing in their day, these volumes effectively created the aircraft 'picture book' market through the ideal marriage of professional photography and top quality printing in a competitively priced package.

The editor behind the series was the youthful Dennis Baldry, who was 'head-hunted' by Osprey from *Flight International* in 1982. A true aviation enthusiast, he was employed with the brief to expand the aviation list as rapidly as possible in order to take a share of the lucrative US market. With North America firmly in mind, the first few titles commissioned by Dennis focused on US-related subject matter – *Reno - Air Racing Unlimited* was published in 1983, followed by *Sky Truck* in 1984 and *EAA Oshkosh* in 1985. All three volumes also had

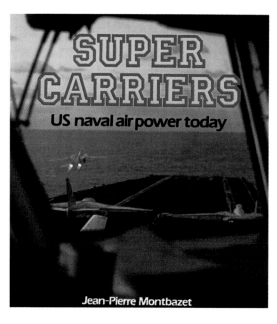

one other thing in common. They were written and photographed by former *Flight International* colleagues of the Editor in the form of Nigel Moll and the late Stephen Piercey.

These books quickly proved the soundness of the package, with the *Sky Truck* volume reprinting twice in subsequent years following its publication. Aside from enjoying commercial success, the early titles also garnered 'official' recognition from no less a body than the Aviation/Space Writers Association of America, who judged Nigel Moll's colourful *Reno - Air Racing Unlimited* the winner of both the prestigious National Photography and Earl D Osborn awards for general aviation journalism in 1983.

The inspiration behind the author's career choice – the most successful Osprey Colour Series book ever published, *SUPER CARRIERS* by Parisian television journalist Jean-Pierre Montbazet. Over 26,000 copies of this book were sold, and it received rave reviews. The following selected extract was taken from the review by Jan Jacobs, which appeared in the Winter 1985 edition of the US naval aviation journal, *The Hook*;

'This book is probably one of the best photo essays of modern navy carrier air power. For the sheer art of the photography within the covers, this book is worth the price. For the added bonus of being about navy carriers, this one becomes a must-have for any Tailhook member'

The recipe followed by Dennis Baldry and Osprey with the Colour Series was stunningly simple. Pick an action-packed subject, commission a professional aviation photojournalist to go and cover it from all angles with his Nikons, Canons or Bronicas, and then select around 130 of his best photographs for inclusion in an all-colour volume sympathetically designed to give these images the most impact.

Printed in Hong Kong on good quality gloss-art paper stock, the finished product was made available to aviation enthusiasts at a price that was only marginally more expensive than the cost of a quality monthly aircraft magazine at that time. And no aviation periodicals were all-colour then either.

Colour Series books were also appreciably cheaper than the competition in virtually all english-language markets across the globe, with Osprey being able to keep the price down thanks to print runs of between 6000 and 8000 copies per title.

AUSTRALIAN CONNECTION

Living in far off Perth, Western Australia, at the time the Osprey publishing 'revolution' was just gaining momentum, my first real introduction to the Colour Series came in the form of the original *Super Carriers - US naval air power today*, published in 1985. A truly remarkable piece of photojournalism, this book was filled from cover to cover with images of carrier operations taken by author Jean-Pierre Montbazet in the Mediterranean during his six visits to CV/CVNs between 1981 and 1984.

The photographs in this volume struck a particular chord with me, as my local port of Fremantle often played host to US carrier battlegroups enjoying a well-earned week of 'R&R' following long periods on 'Gonzo Patrol' at the entrance to the Persian Gulf.

I regularly visited these vessels whilst they were either in port, or swinging at anchor just a mile or two off the coast in Gage Roads. Through access to such ships, and the 70+ aircraft embarked, my developing passions for photography and military aviation were regularly satisfied, although I harboured a burning desire to witness 'blue water ops'. I soon realised that the only way I was going to achieve this was to somehow garner a book contract from a publisher. Sadly, my credentials at that point were less than extensive, my experience in the area of photo-journalism consisting of just the first year in a three-year English course that I was in the process of completing at Curtin University.

However, the publication of *Super Carriers* inspired me to write to Osprey in search of a book contract on the principal of 'nothing ventured, nothing gained'. Having subsequently managed the company's aviation list both as a full-time employee and, since 1994, in a freelance capacity, I have received countless letters identical to mine from individuals across the globe seeking to produce books for Osprey. Sadly, most of these have not resulted in the issuing of contracts.

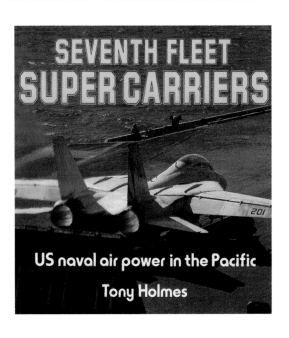

My first effort in the world of aviation publishing. *SEVENTH FLEET SUPERCARRIERS* was published in November 1987, and enjoyed a single reprint the following year

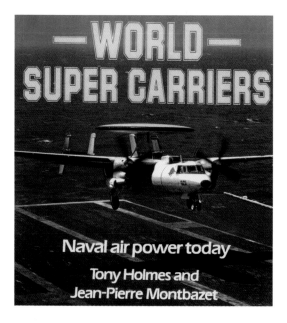

Despite having never met Jean-Pierre Montbazet, we collaborated for the final Colour Series book to carry the *Super Carriers* title. This volume, which included aircraft and ships from Britain and France, as well as US Navy and Marine Corps assets, was published in the summer of 1988

Indeed, it was only after I had written a good number of rejection letters that the full impact of the decision made in February 1986 by my predecessor, Dennis Baldry, struck home. He had taken a huge gamble by commissioning a total novice from the other side of the world to produce a follow-on volume to what would eventually become the best-selling Colour Series book of all time. Yes, *Super Carriers* sold a staggering 26,000+ copies in its original form, being reprinted three times in as many years.

My pitch to Osprey had centred on the fact that *Monsieur* Montbazet's tome had focused almost exclusively on east coast carriers operating with the Sixth Fleet in the Mediterranean. The Seventh Fleet was my local force, and their 'patch' covered most of the Western Pacific and all of the Indian Ocean. Usually, only west coast carriers undertake deployments with the Seventh Fleet, so the opportunity for duplicating Montbazet's work by covering the same air wings was remote.

Aside from offering coverage of suitably different aircraft and carriers, I also had another 'ace up my sleeve' when it came to convincing Osprey to take a punt on this 'Young Turk' from 'Downunder' – Capt Ross H Underhill, Commander, US Seventh Fleet Representative in Western Australia.

A three-tour Vietnam 'vet', Capt Underhill had seen combat in A-4C/E Skyhawks with VA-153 'Blue Tail Flies' from USS *Constellation* (CVA 64) in 1966 and *Coral Sea* (CVA 43) in 1967-68, followed by A-7A Corsair IIs again with the same unit in 1970, this time from USS *Oriskany* (CVA 34). He was the real 'mover and shaker' behind the US Navy agreeing to my request to visit carriers at sea, which in turn convinced my Editor of the feasibility of my proposal. *Seventh Fleet Super Carriers* was 'good to go'.

AT SEA

Having been given clearance for a series of embarks, my first exposure to deck ops came in July 1986 when I flew aboard USS *Enterprise* (CVN 65). Armed with my trusty Chinon CM-3, my father's slightly more modern Olympus OM10 and the grand total of six rolls of Kodachrome 64, I spent the next two days in military aviation heaven, watching Air Wing Eleven (CVW-11) 'flex its muscles' over the bombing ranges along the coast of Western Australia.

Five months later I photographed the now-defunct Air Wing Fifteen (CVW-15) as it operated from the deck of USS *Carl Vinson* (CVN 70) whilst the carrier headed south for Fremantle at the end of its *WestPac*. I now required just one more embark to complete the photography for the book, and with no vessels due in local waters until late 1987, I had to head north to the Japanese island of Okinawa in order to fulfil my contractual obligations. What awaited me was USS *Ranger* (CV 61), sailing in the Sea of Japan following her participation in Exercise *Team Spirit '87*. Having successfully 'shot' the vessel's unique all-Grumman CVW-2 as it went about its business conducting surge operations with various allied forces in the region, I returned to Perth with *Seventh Fleet Super Carriers* at last in the can.

The book went on sale in late 1987, and I am glad to say that it sold in sufficient numbers to enjoy a single reprint. My second volume, *World Super Carriers*, was co-authored with Jean-Pierre Montbazet and released in 1988. Since then, I have been fortunate enough to enjoy full-time employment in the world of aviation publishing, working predominantly for Osprey, but also for a number of other publishers in the UK and USA. My most recent carrier tome, *Combat Carriers*, was co-published by Airlife and Motorbooks International in 1998, and has since appeared in Czech and German language editions.

THE PAST, THE PRESENT AND THE FUTURE

Since the first aviation Colour Series volume appeared in 1983, Osprey has released more than 100 titles that could be termed 'picture books'. The all-colour format, which emphasises photographs over words, has been imitated by countless publishers worldwide, and has also attracted criticism from certain reviewers whom, I feel, have missed the point of these books.

At worst, the Colour Series (and volumes of this type in general) has served as a modestly-priced entry-level list of titles for those individuals becoming aware of aviation, and more importantly aviation publishing, for the first time. At best, they have served to document a facet of military, civil or warbird aviation that is no longer with us today. As I sit at my desk and flick through my bent and battered file copy of *Seventh Fleet Super Carriers*, the latter aspect comes to the fore time and again as I see squadrons (VF-1, VF-114 and VAW-114 to name but three), a ship (the *Ranger*) and aircraft types

such as the Intruder, Corsair II and Sea King that are no longer a part of today's US Navy.

Returning to the present day, you hold in your hands my latest volume for Osprey, which features photographs taken during visits to US carriers between September 1997 and June 1999. In an effort to recreate the flavour of classic Colour Series books of the 1980s, I have split the aircraft types up generically and produced detailed captions for each photograph, rather than a continuous body text that runs throughout each chapter. Carefully selected first-hand accounts from naval aviators are liberally sprinkled within the captions, and these reveal aspects of modern 'blue water ops' that are rarely detailed in books of this type. Finally, a concise appendix features a full BuNo listing for those aircraft embarked during my visits.

Well, that is enough of my personal ramblings. It's time to fasten the chin strap on your cranial, button up your 'float coat' and pull down your goggles in preparation for a flightdeck-level view of modern US naval aviation in action.

Go Navy!

Tony Holmes
Sevenoaks, Kent
April 2000

TOP CAT

◀ Hook down, wings fully swept back and afterburner nozzles 'puckered', VF-31's 'Tomcat 102' lines up for a fast pass along the starboard side of the USS *Abraham Lincoln* (CVN 72). The pilot will level the fighter off at 800 ft above the sea, run by the ship and, once past the bow, 'break' into a tight 4g turn to port at 400 mph and descend to 600 ft in order to enter the landing pattern. He then commences his landing configuration checks, 'dirtying up' the jet in the crosswind turn by lowering the landing gear and flaps whilst flying a continuous curving arc during the downwind leg of his recovery *(Photo by Cdr Tom Twomey)*

▼ Once in the final stages of his landing approach, the pilot should find himself lined up with the carrier's angled deck around three-quarters of a mile aft of the ship. In radio communication with the Landing Signal Officer (LSO) throughout the final phase of the flight, he 'rides' the centred 'meatball' of the OLS (Optical Landing System) right onto the deck of the carrier. This colourfully-marked F-14D (BuNo 164600) is seen just seconds away from slamming back down onto the deck of CVN 72 during CVW-14's CompTUEx (Competitive Training Unit Exercise) in the SoCal (Southern California) Ops area in late November 1997. 'Tomcat 100' had initially been delivered by Grumman to West Coast F-14 Fleet Readiness Squadron (FRS) VF-124 at NAS Miramar, California, in early 1992. It was in turn passed on to VF-101 Det Miramar (also known as 'Det West') following the disbandment of the former unit in September 1994. The fighter became the Commander Air Group (CAG) 'bird' of VF-31 'Tomcatters' in late 1997, replacing BuNo 163893, which was issued to VF-213 'Black Lions' at this time following the latter unit's conversion to F-14Ds *(Photo by Cdr Tom Twomey)*

▶ Two months prior to the November 1997 CompTUEx, VF-31 had flown four jets from NAS Oceana to the SoCal Ops area in order to join the rest of CVW-14 aboard CVN 72. The primary purpose of this 'mini det' was to get eight recently-arrived junior officers deck qualified in the Tomcat in advance of the squadron-strength deployment for the CompTUEx. Led by VF-31's boss at the time, Cdr Michael C 'Nasty' Manazir, and his RIO (Radar Intercept Officer), all five crews successfully gained their deck 'quals' during a fortnight of cyclic ops as part of the wing's Tailored Ship's Training Assessment (TSTA) II/III phase. Here, 'Tomcatter 110' (BuNo 159618) is carefully positioned on deck elevator four following the completion of a sortie. This aircraft was originally delivered to the navy as an A-model as long ago as October 1975, being issued to VF-124 on the 24th of that month. The penultimate D-model upgrade, it became the 17th of 18 F-14D(R)s to be remanufactured when it was converted by Grumman during the course of 1991

▶ Seen on the opening spread of this chapter, 'Tomcatter 102' (alias F-14D BuNo 164344) is manoeuvred into position by tractor near the stern of CVN 72 during the TSTA-II/-III period. Delivered new to VF-124 in October 1991, the Tomcat was passed on to VF-31 the following year, and is still on strength with the unit today

▶ A typical air wing in the US Navy of the new millennium will include a single squadron of Tomcats equipped with ten aircraft. The jet is old and labour-intensive (currently, 60+ maintenance hours are required for every one flying hour), and both the unit's 150-strong maintenance department and the ship's Aircraft Maintenance Division (AIMD) work long shifts to keep at least six of the ten embarked aircraft serviceable at any one time. When flying in the Persian Gulf as part of the US Navy's commitment to Operation *Southern Watch* (OSW), a standard naval package will usually include two Tomcats, which are capable of performing a variety of roles from fighter escort to FastFAC. In order for two F-14s to fly 'over the beach' into Iraqi airspace, a third aircraft is always launched to act as an aerial 'spare' should one of the primary jets suffer a technical fault. The navy strives to train in much the same way as it would fight, and so when cyclic ops are underway, a typical evolution will see three Tomcats launch as part of a 'mixed bag' of around 15 to 20 aircraft. Returning after a training sortie over the Persian Gulf in early March 1999, this trio of F-14Ds from VF-213 'Black Lions' are seen just as the leader has pulled up and pitched left into the landing pattern above USS *Carl Vinson* (CVN 70). His wingmen will follow him into the break at precise 15-second intervals

▼ 'Blacklion 111' is carefully lined up with the cat track for waist cat three prior to being launched on an early evening sortie from CVN 70. One of three ex-F-14A 'retreads' within VF-213, BuNo 161159 has the distinction of being the first A-model remanufactured as an F-14D(R). This work was undertaken by Grumman at Bethpage, in New York, in the later half of 1990. The veteran jet had originally been delivered to the navy on 25 April 1981, and served for many years with VF-32 prior to its rebuild. Upon the aircraft's return to the fleet, the Tomcat initially flew with VF-31, before transferring to VF-213 in late 1997

◄ Firmly attached to waist cat three, 'Blacklion 106' is in the final stages of preparation for launch. The fighter carries a single AIM-54C Phoenix missile mounted snugly in the forward port centreline pallet, as well as a solitary AIM-9M Sidewinder on the wing glove pylon. With such a 'load-out', the crew of this aircraft can cover both the long- and short-range threats which may oppose the OSW package that they are protecting during its 'Vul time' (period of Vulnerability) in 'the box' over southern Iraq. VF-213 made history by firing two half-ton 'Buffaloes' – the crews' nickname for the AIM-54 – during the unit's 1998-99 deployment in the Gulf with CVW-11. The missiles were launched against Iraqi aircraft (reportedly MiG-25s) violating the no-fly zone on 5 January 1999, this mission marking the first time that the AIM-54 had been fired in combat in 25 years of service with the navy. The crews involved took the missile shots at extreme range, and although both rounds missed their targets due to the MiGs turning back north, it is believed that one of the Iraqi interceptors subsequently crashed due to fuel exhaustion

▶ The green-shirted hook-up crewman for bow cat two checks the nose gear's hydraulic retraction jack on 'Blacklion 107' (BuNo 163903) prior to declaring the 70,000-lb fighter fit for launching. VF-213 was kept incredibly busy whilst in the Gulf, flying 70 OSW air-to-air and air-to-ground missions (230 sorties), totalling in excess of 615 combat hours. Some 19 strikes were carried out, with 20 laser-guided bombs (LGBs) being expended for a 64 per cent success rate, whilst a further 11 combined strikes were supported by the unit. Additionally, 45 reconnaissance overflights of southern Iraq were also successfully completed, with more than 580 targets 'imaged' by TARPS (Tactical Air Reconnaissance Pod System) configured F-14Ds. During my visit to CVN 70, the crews in VF-213 seemed to be more than happy with the sortie rate that the unit was being asked to maintain. One RIO told me;

'Everybody is flying at least once a day at the moment, sometimes twice, so we are all getting plenty of air time. That said, OSW missions are not what they used to be – continuous patrols for hours on end, day after day. Now we fly a short, focused, mission as part of a strike package, hit a target, and come out. However, the mission planning is considerably more complex than in the old days'

▶ 'Blacklion 106' (BuNo 159619) 'sits' just short of waist cat three, its nose gear in the 'kneeled' launching position and nose tow bar down. The aircraft will shortly be motioned forward onto the cat track by a yellow-shirted plane director, the tow bar's T-shaped end slotting into the rectangular 'box' visible in the track immediately ahead of the bar. The cat shuttle will then retract back down the length of the catapult until in the correct position to engage the tow bar, and once they have been successfully mated, the Tomcat is put into tension for launch by the pilot advancing the throttle to military power. From this head-on view, the F-14D's distinctive Lockheed Martin Electric/Northrop dual undernose sensor pod, housing a Lockheed Martin AN/AAS-42 Infra-Red Scanner/Tracker (IRST – domed on the right) and Northrop AN/AAX-1 Television Camera Set (TCS – flat on the left), can be clearly seen. On the underside of the pod is a red anti-collision light which has been 'scabbed' onto the front of the housing for the AN/ALQ-165 Radar Homing and Warning System (RHAWS) antenna. This particular jet was the ninth F-14A converted into a D-model, being remanufactured by Grumman in 1991 and then issued to VX-4 for Electromagnetic Environmental Effects testing. It was subsequently passed on to VF-2 in February 1994, who in turn sent it to VF-31 in late 1996. The Tomcat joined it present unit in early 1998. Part of the US Navy inventory since October 1975, BuNo 159619 had previously served with VF-124, VF-24 and VF-1 prior to its remanufacture

▶ Whilst the shuttle pulls the F-14 down the catapult with breakneck acceleration, the white hold-back bar that has held the aircraft in position lies motionless in the catapult groove. This device effectively restrains the aircraft until the 'repeatable release' hydraulic hold-back (contained within the bar) gives way when the prede-termined load exerted on it by the combined force of the catapult and the aircraft's engines can no longer be withstood. This force is calculated to be sufficient to enable the jet to successfully launch. 'Blacklion 107' will be travelling at 150 knots by the time it reaches the end of the catapult, some 300 ft down the deck – and just two seconds after the launch button has been pressed by bow cat two's 'shooter'. The D-model is cleared for non-afterburner launches only, its twin General Electric F110-GE-400s being capable of propelling a fully-laden 71,000-lb Tomcat away from the carrier in military-rated power. The F-14A, however, requires Zone Three afterburner to remain airborne after leaving the catapult

▲ With the removal of all naval aircraft from NAS Miramar in 1997, and the posting off all west coast-based F-14 units several thousand miles east to NAS Oceana, Commander Naval Air Forces Pacific (COMNAVAIRPAC) was left with just one permanently assigned frontline Tomcat unit within its ranks. – VF-154 'Black Knights'. Aside from this solitary distinction, the squadron is also unique in being the only forward-deployed F-14 unit in the navy, sharing its base at NAF Atsugi, near Tokyo, with the eight other squadrons that form CVW-5. Despite their 'overseas' status, and equipment with 11 venerable F-14As, VF-154 proved their ability during virtually back-to-back deployments to the Persian Gulf in 1998-99. The successful completion of such a gruelling operational schedule resulted in the 'Black Knights' winning no less than five major awards from three separate commands. The ultimate prize was the Chief of Naval Operations' Joseph C Clifton award, which marked VF-154 out as being the finest fighter squadron in the navy. The unit also received COMNAVAIRPAC's Battle Efficiency 'E' and 'Boola-Boola' award for air warfare excellence, whilst its maintenance team earned the Golden Wrench from Combat Fighter Wing Atlantic (COMFITWINGLANT), and combined with VF-154's flight crews to secure the Safety 'S'. Here, 'Nite 102' (BuNo 161280) is held by the catapult officer for bow cat one prior to it launching from USS Kitty Hawk (CV 63) in the Persian Gulf in late June 1999

▲ Just seconds later, 'Nite 102' closes on the bow of CV 63, propelled down the deck through a combination of catapult power and raw thrust from the aircraft's twin Pratt & Whitney TF30-P-414A turbofan engines in Zone Three afterburner. The veteran Tomcat has proven to be one of CVW-5's primary assets during its recent OSW deployments, with the CAG, Capt Rick McHarg, being particularly appreciative of its ability as a bomber;

'As an ex-A-6 BN (Bombardier-Navigator), when it comes to finding the target in a FLIR-equipped F-14, and then hitting it with an LGB, the Tomcat is a superior platform to the Intruder. This is principally because the LANTIRN pod is GPS-driven. Backing up this precision bombing capability, our F-14s also have all the latest electronic warning equipment installed, as well as FTI (Fast Tactical Imagery). The latter system allows VF-154 to send TARPS imagery back to the ship over a range of around 120 miles through the jet's UHF radios'

▲ Aside from each aircraft carrying its own nickname, VF-154's Tomcats also wore various letters and emblems denoting their numerous awards. Clustered beneath the pilot's cockpit can be seen a Safety 'S' and Battle Efficiency 'E', split by the Golden Wrench. Immediately below this is the word *Clifton*, denoting VF-154's status as the best fighter unit in the navy, whilst to the left of the 'E' is a silhouette of a Phoenix missile, which is the traditional symbol for the 'Boola-Boola' award. Of this trio, *Tina Rose* (BuNo 161280/102) is the oldest, having been delivered to VF-101 from Grumman in April 1981. It subsequently served with VF-31, VF-103, VF-102 (with whom it saw action in Operation *Desert Storm*) and then VF-101 again, before spending time in storage at NAS Jacksonville. The jet was duly upgraded as part of the F-14MMCAP (Multi-Mission Capability Avionics Program), which saw the AN/ALR-67 Radar Warning Receiver (RWR) system fitted; the aircraft made compatible with the LAU-7 missile launcher rail/CelsiusTech BOL chaff dispenser; installation of a Programmable Tactical Information Display (PTID) in the rear cockpit; modification of the venerable analogue 5400 mission computer with digital capabilities from the F-14D's AN/AYK-14 system; and the addition of twin Military Standard 1553B databases. Following this upgrading, BuNo 161280 was sent to VF-154 in early 1998 as part of the unit's re-equipment with improved F-14As. *El Diablo II* (BuNo 162697/106) was issued to the navy in August 1986, serving with VF-32 and VF-41, before its assignment to VF-154 in 1998. *Duke* (BuNo 162592/105) was accepted straight from Bethpage by VF-1 in January 1986, and went on to fly with VF-51 and VF-21 prior to its allocation to VF-154 in late 1997

▲ Named after the wife of VF-154's MMCO (Maintenance Material Control Officer), Lt(jg) Joey Vargas, *Mi Evy* (BuNo 161293) zeros in on the worn deck of CV 63, its crew braced for the 'trap' which will see the big fighter decelerate from 123 knots to a dead stop in around two seconds, and 300 ft. Pilots assigned to CVW-5 have to be amongst the best 'stick and rudder' men in the navy, due to the lack of opportunity for carrier landing practice in Japan. 'Black Knight' pilot Lt(jg) Guillermo 'Ace'N' Geary explains;

'To secure a posting to Air Wing Five you have graduate from the FRS with a Priority A classification, which means that you have done well when undergoing Carrier Qualifications (CQs). I would say that the A-model Tomcat pilots are generally better at their job than their B- and D-model counterparts simply because they have to work harder in the baseline jet, particularly around the boat.'

Working hard in his 17-year-old fleet veteran, the pilot of 'Nite 103' is look good for an 'OK' three-wire grading from the Landing Signals Officer (LSO) – and a highly sought after green block on the 'Greenie Board', on display in VF-154's ready room one level below the flightdeck

▲ *El Diablo II* arrives back aboard CV 63 with a resounding thud. Naval aviators are taught to continue their landing at the same rate of descent and angle of attack until the aircraft meets the deck, for this is the only way to place the tailhook accurately in amongst the four wires spaced some 40 feet apart at the stern of the carrier

◀ *Animal* (BuNo 161617) is steered by its pilot towards bow cat one. This aircraft carries a LANTIRN pod on Station 8B, while above it is a live AIM-9M affixed to a combined LAU-7 missile launcher rail/Celsius Tech BOL chaff dispenser. As with all other LANTIRN-equipped Tomcat units assigned to OSW, VF-154 has enjoyed great success with the bolt-on system. One of those to use it in action in 1999 was RIO, Lt(jg) Rich 'Bean' Hill;

'Despite the age of our jets, the squadron has done some excellent work on this cruise. We have consistently dropped LGBs right in the "pickle barrel" when called upon to do so, proving the value of LANTIRN. Indeed, the addition of this pod currently makes the F-14 the best bombing platform in the navy.'

BuNo 161617 was originally delivered new to VF-154's long-time sister-squadron VF-21 when the unit switched from Phantom IIs to Tomcats in late 1983. It then spent time with the Pacific Missile Test Center at NAS Point Mugu, in California, before rejoining the fleet with VF-111. Upon the disestablish-ment of the latter unit at NAS Miramar in March 1995, the jet was assigned to VF-213, before joining VF-154 in mid-1997. The acronym *BKR* at the base of the tail fin stands for 'Black Knights Rule', this marking being instigated in 1998 by the unit's then CO, Cdr Drew 'Bluto' Brugal

◀ All nine F-14s that survived CVW-5's *WestPac* of 1999 looked less than pristine by the end of their third month on the line in the Persian Gulf. The tenth jet embarked, BuNo 161299 (modex '101'), was lost as a result of mechanical failure on the night of 15 June 1999 when its pilot – the Operations Officer for CVW-5 – had one engine fail and the second refuse to come out of afterburner whilst in flight. He attempted to land the crippled fighter back aboard CV 63, but after several attempts realised that he could not handle the Tomcat accurately enough to effect a recovery. 'CAG Ops' was then instructed to refuel from the duty S-3B tanker and head for a shore base, but again the jet proved unmanageable around the drogue. With the fighter's fuel state now critically low, the crew was forced to abandon the Tomcat, and following a successful ejection, they were both swiftly 'fished out' of the Persian Gulf by the Plane Guard Seahawk and returned to the carrier. Fortunately, *Mi Evy* suffered no such mishaps during the deployment, and is seen here under tension in preparation for launch. Like the rest of VF-154's jets, this aircraft received the F-14MMCAP upgrade at NAS Jacksonville in 1998 prior to being issued to the unit

LIGHT STRIKE

► Since the late 1980s, the McDonnell Douglas (now Boeing) F/A-18 Hornet has dominated the flightdecks of the US Navy's fleet of CV/CVNs. Today, the composition of most air wings includes three squadrons of Hornets, totalling some 36+ jets – or more than half the aircraft typically embarked on a carrier. Jets from two of the three light strike units aboard USS *Abraham Lincoln* (CVN 72) as part of CVW-14 are seen parked in the area dubbed the 'Crotch' by plane directors working the deck during the vessel's TSTA-II/-III phase in September 1997. The middle aircraft ('Sting 311', alias BuNo 164686) is assigned to the navy's senior fleet-going Hornet unit, VFA-113, whilst the jets flanking it ('Talon 205'/BuNo 163458 and 'Talon 207'/BuNo 163481) belong to one of the newest F/A-18 squadrons, VFA-115. CVW-14 was enjoying its first taste of 'at sea' operations aboard CVN 72 during my visit, its various squadrons having been ashore for almost a year prior to this following the completion of their previous *WestPac* aboard CVN 70 in November 1996. Due to their extended period on land, most of the embarked aircraft looked immaculate

◄ Nicknamed the 'Eagles', for many years VFA-115 had flown A-6 Intruders with CVW-5 in Japan prior to transitioning to early-build C-model Hornets (obtained primarily from VFA-81 and -83) in 1996-97. The unit was then sent to CVW-14, where it replaced the disestablished VA-196 – the last Intruder squadron in AIRPAC. In order to transition the 'new' VFA-115 onto Hornets in the quickest possible time, a number of ex-F/A-18 pilots were drafted into the unit, as Cdr Andy 'Maddog' McCawley, CO of fellow light strike squadron VFA-113, explained to me;

'When the navy stood up VFA-115, it made sure that it had staffed all the senior positions within the unit with senior guys, rather than just transitioning all the A-6 pilots to Hornets, leaving the new squadron "behind the power curve" in the air wing work-ups. Sure, just like us, the squadron also had a lot of new guys come in, but the Operations Officer, Training Officer, Executive Officer and most of the other department heads were ex-Hornet men'.

F/A-18C BuNo 163439 was marked up as the unit's 'CAG bird', wearing the traditional black tails of CVW-14, along with a rendition of the air wing badge on the inside of its twin fins. The 12th production-standard C-model built by McDonnell Douglas, this Lot X aircraft served for many years with VFA-83, prior to being sent to VFA-115 in 1997 following the former unit's transition to brand new Lot XIX and XX Hornets at around the same time

▲ VFA-113's 'CAG bird' (BuNo 164640) also wore high-visibility markings to denote its special status, boasting the name of CAG, Capt Tom 'Killer' Kilcline, beneath the cockpit on the left-hand side of the jet, and Deputy CAG (D-CAG), Capt Harvey 'H-Mac' MacDonald, on the right. During CVW-14's subsequent *WestPac '98* deployment, D-CAG MacDonald passed the significant career milestone of 1000 'traps', this event taking place on 9 August when he recovered aboard CVN 72 in a VFA-25 jet whilst operating in the Persian Gulf

▶ 'CAG birds' have worn numerous markings over the years, with most being a rainbow-coloured variation of the squadron emblem worn by the remaining aircraft in the unit. Multi-shaded markings first came into vogue in the late 1940s, with each colour representing the different squadrons within the air wing. With the advent of the Tactical Paint Scheme (TPS), some units have abandoned the rainbow in favour of a colour rendition of their emblem, but VFA-113 have stuck with tradition and adorned 'Sting 300' with this vibrant marking for the past decade

▶ The third Hornet unit within CVW-14 in 1997 was VFA-25 which, like VFA-113, received the first F/A-18s issued to the US Navy way back in 1983 when it transitioned from A-7E Corsair IIs. Since then, the 'Fist of the Fleet' has completed seven *WestPac* deployments with the aircraft, experiencing sea time aboard USS *Constellation* (CV 64), USS *Independence* (CV 62) and USS *Carl Vinson* (CVN 70), prior to following CVW-14 to the *Abraham Lincoln* in 1997. Parked in the area known as 'Point' to the plane directors, two VFA-25 jets ('CAG bird' BuNo 164633 and BuNo 164654) and 'Talon 204' (BuNo 163456) can be seen undergoing their final preparations for the next round of cyclic ops. Thanks to the aircraft's relative youthfulness in comparison with other air wing types such as the Tomcat, Prowler or Viking, the Hornet has by far the lowest maintenance hours per flying hour figure of any fixed-wing combat aircraft on the flightdeck today – around 20 to 1. This compares with 60+ to 1 for the Tomcat!

▶ Sting 312' (BuNo 164220) was the oldest jet in VFA-113 at the time of my visit to CVN 72, this Lot XIV aircraft having been transferred into the unit from west coast FRS VFA-125 in the summer of 1997 – the bulk of the 'Stingers' remaining Hornets had been delivered to the squadron in 1991-92. A close inspection of the jet reveals a Lockheed Martin AN/ASQ-173 LST/SCAM (Laser Spot Tracker/Strike CAMera) affixed to station six – the starboard 'shoulder' pylon – between the intake and the 330-US gal external tank. Lt 'Zeno' Rausa, formerly of VFA-94 and now with VFA-122, explained to me how this system worked;

'This device scans for laser energy within its field of view (FOV), and once this has been located, the LST points to this spot. From here, the pilot commands a designation that will lock all his sensors to the target, as well as directing steering cues for his weapons on the aircraft's HUD (Head-Up Display). The laser energy it finds can come from three basic sources – internally from the Loral AAS-38B NITE Hawk FLIR-LTD/R pod, from a ground source such as a hand-held laser device (the Marines use these), or from another aircraft such as a Tomcat with a LANTIRN pod or laser-equipped Hornet. Obviously, if you were "lasing" the target yourself, there would be no need for the LST, because you would already know where the target is'

◄ Exhibiting signs of 'wear and tear' following a sustained three-month period on the line supporting OSW, 'Beefeater 314' (BuNo 164012) closes on the hard steel of CVN 70 at the end of yet another gulf flight. To the right of the jet's nose modex is a small stencilled mission marking which denotes that this aircraft dropped a Raytheon AGM-154A Joint Stand-Off Weapon (JSOW) earlier in the deployment. Indeed, one of CVW-11's many 'claims to fame' on this *WestPac* was that its two C-model Hornet units debuted the navy's future precision weapon of choice in combat over Iraq. The first two rounds were expended on the night of 25 January 1999, when a SAM site near Basra was neutralised. This target had proven a thorn in the Coalition's side since the ending of *Desert Storm*, and as with the subsequent 14 JSOWs that were dropped by CVW-11 up to the time of CVN 70's departure from the gulf, all three were categorised as bull's-eye strikes

▶ Ironically, whilst VFA-22 and -94 were debuting the navy's newest weapon in combat, the third Hornet squadron aboard CVN 70 was having to make do with the oldest frontline F/A-18s in the fleet. VFA-97 'Warhawks' (whose garishly-painted BuNo 163143 is seen here) is currently the only frontline unit still flying A-model jets, and although they may appear outwardly identical to any other Hornet wearing the 'NH' tailcode aboard *Carl Vinson*, looks are, in this case, most definitely deceptive. Starting with its powerplant, the A-model still uses the standard General Electric F404-GE-400 turbofan, whereas some C-models now employ the -402 Enhanced Performance Engine (EPE), which has greatly improved levels of static thrust, and better high speed performance at low to medium altitudes. As impressive as the new engines are, the F/A-18C really leaves the A-model trailing in its wake when it comes to the power of its software, systems and avionics, which have bene-fited from continual upgrades throughout the late 1980s and for the duration of the 1990s. The advent of the night-attack Lot XII F/A-18C brought together a host of preci-sion targeting systems with 'smart' ordnance, and this was further improved with equipment such as MSI (Multi-Sensor Integration), the Litton ASN-39 ring-laser-gyro INS (Inertial Navigation System) and the Hughes APG-73 radar. Fitted as standard in Lot XVI to XX jets, this equip-ment has combined to make the C-model a far more versatile fighter-bomber than the appreciably older F/A-18A

◀ Jets from all three Hornet units sit side-by-side over bow cat two – a traditional 'parking area' frequented by light strike squadrons over the decades. Heading this line up is an F/A-18A from VFA-97, equipped with a Texas Instruments AGM-88C Block IV High-speed Anti-Radiation Missile (HARM). A SAM and radar 'busting' weapon without equal, the HARM proved a favourite with CVW-11, for its aircraft fired off no fewer than 20 such missiles against Iraqi targets during Suppression of Enemy Air Defenses (SEAD) missions between December 1998 and April 1999. Since then, the Rules of Engagement (RoE) observed by Coalition aircraft assigned to OSW missions have been tightened in respect to the employment of HARMs, and few such missiles have been fired

◄ The 1998-99 deployment by VFA-97 marked the 19th such occasion that the 'Warhawks' had undertaken a *WestPac*. It was also the first time that the unit had seen combat since January 1973, when it had flown A-7E Corsair IIs over Vietnam as part of CVW-14, embarked on USS *Enterprise* (CVN 65). Whilst committed to OSW, VFA-97 flew more than 150 sorties over southern Iraq, dropping 10,000 lbs of ordnance whilst enforcing the no-fly zone. As with other assets in CVW-11, the unit also participated in the last strikes of Operation *Desert Fox* on 19 December 1998. Waiting for the 'final turn-up' signal from bow cat two's 'shooter', the pilot of 'Warhawk 210' (BuNo 163106) keeps a weather eye on what is occurring on the catapult next to him. This jet is heading out for a little 'in-house' visual bombing training, hence the Mk 76 25-lb 'blue bombs' attached to the solitary Triple Ejector Rack (TER) hanging beneath the starboard wing. Despite their diminutive size, these weapons accurately replicate the ballistic characteristics of a 500-lb Mk 82 'dumb' bomb

▲ Streaming contrails from its wingtips, a Lot XII F/A-18C from VFA-94 approaches the stern of CVN 70 with its tailhook firmly locked down and massive slotted trailing edge flaps and ailerons fully 'drooped'. The leading edge flaps have also been deployed, and like the wing's other moveable surfaces, they are computer programmed to deflect for optimum lift at the reduced airspeeds associated with landing

◄ Maintenance crews from VFA-97 fuss over their charges parked on the 'crotch' between cycles. 'Warhawk 200' has had its cockpit powered up through the use of an external power source, the cable for which can be seen plugged into the socket to the left of the 'star and bar'. Both aircraft also have their M61A-1 cannon access bay doors ajar. Although these Lot VIII and IX F/A-18As were all delivered to the navy in 1986-87, and are essentially day/visual bombers only due to their inability to use JSOW or JDAMs (or AMRAAM in the fighter role), they can neverthe-less perform a fair proportion of the fighter and strike roles assigned to the Hornet within CVW-11. Former VFA-113 boss, Cdr Andy 'Maddog' McCawley, felt that the older Hornet still had much to offer the fleet when interviewed in September 1997;

'The C-model is much better than the A-model from a functionality perspective, which allows the radar to perform more effectively with newer weapons such as AMRAAM. Having said that, the older Lot VIIIs that I flew in *Desert Storm* were nonetheless very capable, despite lacking some of the "Gucci" stuff that we have now. Granted, the F/A-18C has better operability when involved in a limited action such as OSW, but by Day 15 of any fully blown conflict you will be dropping general purpose bombs on targets, and the A-model Hornet can do this just as effectively as the F/A-18C'

► In a moment of rare coincidence, the actual named pilot of F/A-18A BuNo 163143, Lt Cdr N P 'Waylon' Jennings, is seen signalling to his plane captain that he is about to fire up 'his' jet's second F402-GE-400 turbofan. With the assistance of a 'huffer' start cart, the right powerplant is always started first, followed a short while later by the left engine. With both idling correctly, the pilot will then check his radios (and intercom) and scroll through the built-in test equipment (BITE) to ensure that the myriad systems in his jet are all working as advertised. 'Warhawk 203's' unique colour scheme denotes its previous assignment to the Naval Strike and Air Warfare Center (NSAWC) at NAS Fallon, Nevada. Whilst at the latter facility it wore the modex '34' and carried the combined gunsight (from the old Navy Fighter Weapons School motif) and lightning (ex-'Strike Warfare Center) emblem on its twin fins. This aircraft was assigned to VFA-97 soon after CVW-11 had departed the USA aboard CVN 70 on its *WestPac* in the first week of November 1998, the jet replacing a 'grey' F/A-18A that had suffered a massive engine failure at NAS Lemoore just prior to the unit embarking

► As is traditional amongst all fleet-going squadrons in the US Navy, VFA-94's 'CAG bird' wore flashes of colour to denote its assignment to CVW-11's commanding officer, Capt James T Knight, who was replaced by D-CAG, Capt William A Pokorny, in March 1999 – the latter's name is visible on the starboard side of 'Hobo 400' (BuNo 164066). Photographed during a rare CQ period, when the pilot worked the deck in a series of traps and launches for over 30 minutes, the storeless jet has detailed 'Mighty Shrike' markings picked out in its 'house' colours of black and orange. This Lot XII aircraft has served exclusively with VFA-94 since the unit transitioned from Corsair IIs to Hornets in mid-1990, the 'Mighty Shrikes' being one of the first AirPac units to receive the night-attack capable F/A-18C directly from McDonnell Douglas. This jet swapped modexes with BuNo 164048 in mid-1998, with the latter jet becoming 'Hobo 410'

▲ 'Hobo 411' (BuNo 164027) has its fuel tanks replenished by a purple-shirted 'grape' (aviation fuelling crewman), who has run a hose out from one of the 26 refuelling stations located in the catwalks that surround the deck of CVN 70. Bolted onto the outer starboard wing pylon is an AGM-154A JSOW, which made its combat debut with this unit in January 1999. VFA-94 as a unit pulled together when it came to integrating the weapon into CVN 70's warfighting capabilities, and Lt 'Zeno' Rausa was a 'player' in that team. He was also an active participant in the first operational delivery of JSOW;

'It was fitting that VFA-94 led the first strike, for we had worked hard as a unit to see the weapon attain operational status within CVW-11. Having corrected several systems interface anomalies prior to JSOW — being shipped out to us, we then trained up CAG, D-CAG and all of the CAG "staffers", as well as the personnel in our sister-F/A-18C squadron, VFA-22. We also instructed all pertinent CVN 70 personnel in CVIC (Carrier Intelligence Center) on how to load mission-critical data for the Hornet's weapons delivery computer. The end result of all this hard work was that VFA-94 dropped 10 of the 17 JSOWs used during CVW-11's time on station in the Persian Gulf – and all 17 successfully hit their designated targets'

▲ Although most units adorn their aircraft with personal emblems usually inspired by their squadron badge, the 'Warhawks' of VFA-97 have consistently chosen not to embellish their jets with motifs derived from their insignia (a trident-brandishing bird of prey). Instead, CVW-11's 'NH' code dominates the twin fins of its A-model jets, with the marking on 'Warhawk 200' (BuNo 162835) being applied in full squadron colours

▶ The hook-up crewman keeps his eyes firmly focused on the launch bar as 'Warhawk 200' is motioned forward towards the catapult shuttle on waist cat four. This aircraft was originally delivered to VFA-113 in early 1987 from McDonnell Douglas's St Louis plant, and it remained with the unit until the 'Stingers' transitioned to C-models in early 1990. As one of the last A-7 operators in AirPac, VFA-97 received its first F/A-18Cs in 1991, which it continued to operate until being issued with considerably older A-model Hornets the following year. BuNo 162835 was amongst the latter aircraft passed to the 'Warhawks', and it has served as the unit's 'CAG bird' since 1995

▶ To provide the perfect ending to a well flown sortie, all naval aviators train hard to fly precisely when in full view of the ship, and its crew. The drill for a section or flight recovery is explained by VFA-113 Hornet pilot, Lt Duncan 'Dingo' Clendenin;

'Every squadron derives great pride from slick formation flying over the boat, for this is about the only time that fellow shipmates get to see the aircraft in action. To correctly approach the carrier, you simply follow your formation leader, and once in the pattern, drop down to a height of 800 ft when three miles from the over-head. The leader will aim to fly down the starboard side of the ship, and once you have been given your landing interval in the pattern, the formation will break accordingly – the unit's standard break interval is 17 seconds. A typical approach airspeed is around 350 knots, but if you are coming in for a "shit hot" pass and break, this figure will be much higher – reducing to landing speed from a faster pass can be most interesting! Once you have performed the break, you then set yourself up for landing on the downwind leg to the recovery, and we run the pattern at 600 ft. You are aiming for a 45-second split between aircraft in the formation passing over the ramp'.

This tight four-ship is comprised of aircraft from VFA-22

▼ VFA-22's 'Fighting Redcock' 'CAG bird' (BuNo 164060) clutched the number 50 in its talons aboard CVN 70 in March 1999. This marking was a hangover from the unit's 'half-century' celebration of the previous year, the 'Redcocks' first being established as VF-63 in July 1948. Initially equipped with F8F Bearcats, the unit remained a fighter squadron through to 1956, flying F4U Corsairs, F9F-2/-3 Panthers and F9F-8 Cougars. Redesignated VA-63 in 1956, for the next three years the 'Redcocks' familiarised themselves with the attack mission whilst flying the FJ Fury. In 1959 the unit was renumbered VA-22 and equipped with the A-4 Skyhawk. The 'Redcocks' would subsequently complete no fewer than five combat deployments to Vietnam with the Douglas 'Scooter' (three in C-models and two in Fs) between 1965 and 1970, prior to transitioning to the A-7E the following year. A further two *WestPacs* to South-east Asia were undertaken before US forces finally pulled out of South Vietnam in 1973. The Corsair IIs remained on strength with VA-22 through to 1990, when the first Lot XII F/A-18Cs arrived at the squadron's NAS Lemoore, California, home. Amongst the brand new jets issued to the redesignated VFA-22 was BuNo 164060, which has served as the unit's 'CAG bird' since its allocation to the unit

◄ From one extreme to another! Whereas VFA-22's 'CAG bird' was a small reminder of the glory days of colourful US Navy jets some 30 years ago, the trio of Hornet units embarked on USS *Kitty Hawk* (CV 63) offered the stark contrast of TPS greys, which have blighted naval aviation since the early 1980s. Reflecting their heavy use during the carrier's assignment to OSW in mid-1999, these aircraft had clearly seen a substantial amount of flying. This line up features three Hornets from VFA-27 ('200' modex), two from VFA-192 ('300' modex) and a solitary aircraft from VFA-195 ('400' modex)

▲ Configured for a SEAD (Suppression of Enemy Air Defences) mission as part of a navy OSW package destined to fly into southern Iraq, 'Mace 206' (BuNo 164059) is armed with two AGM-88C Block IV HARMs, two AIM-9L Sidewinders and two belly-mounted AIM-120B AMRAAM. When toting such a 'load out', the Hornet operates closely with the only dedicated electronic warfare (EW) asset in-theatre – the EA-6B Prowler. Although perfectly capable of independently 'sniffing' out and destroying radar and SAM sites thanks to the sensitive seeker and improved processor installed in the HARM, Hornet pilots prefer the shared experience of working with seasoned ECMOs (Electronic Countermeasures Officers) sat in the world's best EW platform. This combination has proven its worth both during and since *Desert Fox*, with the navy firing over 40 HARMs at Iraqi targets in the southern no-fly zone. VFA-27 joined CVW-5 in Japan in mid-1996 following the disbandment of one of the air wing's F-14 units (VF-21) as part of the drawdown of the Tomcat force. This move was good news for VFA-27, for its long-time air wing, CVW-15, had also fallen victim to budget cuts in 1995. As part of the switch, the unit traded in its elderly Lot VIII F/A-18As for Lot XII F/A-18Cs, although this particular aircraft only arrived at NAF Atsugi in 1998, having previously seen service with both VFA-94 and VFA-125

▶ 'Chippy 404' (BuNo 164980) powers towards CV 63's angled deck edge in full afterburner, the aircraft's 'load-out' being deemed heavy enough to warrant this extra 'kick' so as to ensure a safe launch. Aside from the two external drop tanks, this jet is carrying a solitary Mk 82 GBU-12 B/B 500-lb Paveway II LGB on the starboard outer pylon, AIM-9Ms on each wingtip rail and a pair of fuselage-mounted AMRAAMs. The pilot's right hand can also be seen holding onto the catapult grip (dubbed the 'towel rack' by naval aviators) fitted to the canopy rail. This device was installed in order to keep the pilot's hand well away from the control column during the launch stroke, the aircraft's flight control computer instead being given the responsibility of flying the jet off the catapult. It achieves this by commanding nose-up deflection from the fighter's all-moving tailplane. The pilot does, however, retain full control over the throttles, keeping them pushed forward throughout the duration of the launch

▲ Throttles firmly held against the detent in MAX power, the pilot 'sits back and enjoys the ride' as 'Dragon 304' (BuNo 164954) of VFA-192 departs waist cat four in full 'burner. The aircraft's AAS-38B NITE Hawk FLIR-LTD/R pod can be seen affixed to the port shoulder station immediately above the main gear leg. According to VFA-192's CO, Cdr Steve 'Slam' Dunkle, this system makes the Hornet a superior bombing platform to the F-14;

'The FLIR equipment that we use in the Hornet to carry out the same role as the LANTIRN pod-equipped Tomcat is fully integrated into the aeroplane and the weapons system. And by virtue of all the relief modes in the jet, and the seamless integration of the FLIR with the weapons system, the Hornet is a real joy to fly. The F-14 guys can go on about how they have two crew dedicated to the mission in the Tomcat, with the pilot flying the jet and the RIO working the target, but they need both individuals because it is likely that one of the engines in the elderly fighter is not working quite right! Similarly, the jet's LANTIRN capability is essentially derived from a stand-alone weapons system fitted into a pod that is hung on the aeroplane. It is not fully integrated into the F-14's weapons system, and therefore requires the full attention of the RIO in order for it to operate success-fully. You could not slap the same system onto the Hornet without any real integration with its weapons system and expect one guy to run it, as well as fly the aircraft'

► Judging by the appearance of VFA-195's 'Chippy 406' (BuNo 164960), this aircraft had participated in a fair percentage of the 5426 sorties generated by CVW-5! In the early 1980s, when the first TPS grey Tomcat visited an airshow in England, its crew felt it necessary to erect a sign in front of their jet whilst it was parked in the static display area which stated, 'This airplane is not dirty – that's the paint job'. The various squadron maintenance departments and the ship's AIMD personnel are prevented by US naval aviation's bible, NATOPS (Naval Air Training and Operating Procedures Standardization programme), from carrying out overall resprays of aircraft whilst embarked at sea. And with CVW-5 spending more time afloat – eight-and-half-months out of twelve in 1998 – than any other air wing due to its FDNF (Forward-Deployed Naval Forces) status, the end result is an aircraft that looks like this. 'Chippy 406' was one of 12 Lot XVII Hornets that VFA-195 received from CVW-9's VFA-147 in early 1998, the latter unit in return re-equipping with the 'Dambusters'' older Lot XII Hornets. At the same time that this swap was taking place, VFA-192 also completed a similar exchange of aircraft with VFA-147's sister unit, VFA-146. Once the movement of jets had been completed, CVW-5 replaced CVW-9 (aboard the USS *Nimitz* (CVN 68)) on station in the Persian Gulf

◄ Practice bombing mission over (note the storeless TER beneath the starboard wing of the jet), the pilot of 'Dragon 304' snags a four-wire to complete the flying portion of his sortie. Some distance behind him, a section of F-14s close on CV 63 as they prepare to run in and break over the carrier. As with all the air wings that have sailed in these waters since December 1998, CVW-5 completed a number of strikes against targets in Iraq during its three months in the Persian Gulf, with the Hornet very much in the vanguard of these mission;

'"This is not your father's Operation *Southern Watch*", has been the quote for describing the flying all air wings have done in the Gulf post-Operation *Desert Fox*. Since arriving in-theatre we have flown six missions into Iraq that have seen us expending ordnance – most recently night missions employing 2000-lb LGBs. Prior to that, our late model Hornets, which are GPS-equipped, were able to use stand-off weapons like the JSOW, and we enjoyed great success with this system', CAG, Capt Rick McHarg, explained to me in late June 1999. By the time CV 63 was relieved by USS *Theodore Roosevelt* (CVN 71) in early July, CVW-5 had completed 91 days on station and flown 5426 sorties, 1356 of which were over southern Iraq

▲ Seemingly happy in his work, a grinning blue-shirted tractor driver heads slowly towards '1 Row', up on the bow, with his recently-recovered charge, 'Chippy 413' (BuNo 164908). The aircraft's orange wheel chocks are resting on the 'hood' of the tractor, and behind the fighter a further three aircraft can be seen under-tow, their progress being closely monitored by yellow-shirted plane handlers and deck directors. As the jets journey forward, they are 'passed' from one yellow-shirt to the next until they arrive in their allocated spot. The latter are chosen by the Air Boss up in Primary Flight Control ('Pri-Fly'), six stories above the flightdeck. He in turn relays his instructions to the aircraft handling officer ('handler'), who oversees all deck movements from Flight Deck Control, situated at the base of the ship's island

◀ 'Dragon 304' is carefully lined up with bow cat two in preparation for the next cycle of launches. Note the CVW-5 25th anniversary marking worn just aft of the nose modex, and the aircraft's bright yellow main undercarriage legs. The oriental-themed motif was worn on virtually all the aircraft embarked on CV 63 in 1999, whilst the significance of the yellow landing gear remains a mystery to me, as I have never seen the likes of this before on a US navy jet – several other Hornets aboard the ship shared this feature with 'Dragon 304'. The nature of cyclic ops has fundamentally changed over the last 15 years to better suit the Hornet, as 'CAG Five', Capt Rick McHarg, explained to me;

'The evolution of the shorter-range Hornet has made it necessary for us to build our cycle times around this fuel-critical platform. This has had a detrimental impact on the bigger wing Grumman products on deck, which for many years were used to cycles that lasted one hour and forty-five minutes, and missions that lasted for two hours and ten minutes. They are now tied to the shorter schedule, which sees cycle times of between one hour and fifteen minutes and one hour and thirty minutes. The Grumman aircraft can all be ready for the first launch cycle of the day, but once they recover back on deck, it becomes a rush to complete the turn around and fix any problems in time for the next series of flights'

BEAM WEAPONS

▼ Of all the aircraft that comprise a modern carrier air wing, Grumman's EA-6B Prowler is deemed to be one of the most difficult to land thanks to its large size and underpowered Pratt & Whitney J52-P-408A turbojet engines. Just as crew co-ordination is critical in ensuring operational effectiveness when carrying out the EW mission, when it comes to consistently trapping a three-wire 'back at the boat', a similarly close working relationship has to exist between the pilot and ECMO 1, sat 'up front' in the right-hand seat. VAQ-139 NFO, Lt Cdr Scott 'McP' McPherson, explains;

'When recovering, the guys up front divide the workload. Whilst the pilot is flying the aircraft, as ECMO 1, you are responsible for ensuring that all the navigational systems and cockpit displays are working properly. The way the division of work splits up ensures that both the pilot and ECMO 1 are not looking at the same thing at the same time. As his instrument scan is moving around, I have to make sure that my scan is focusing on areas where he may be having a hard time keeping up. This is particularly true when we get to the landing approach. Some pilots like to focus more on their glidepath rather than their azimuth, so the ECMO 1 will help him out with the latter. Others like to adopt a full approach scan, and as an ECMO 1, it is crucial that you jump in and help the pilot out when you see him beginning to struggle to maintain his scan pattern.'

This Block 89 ICAP II Prowler (BuNo 163520) belongs to VAQ-139, and was one of three embarked on CVN 72 for the TSTA-II/-III phase conducted by CVW-14 in September 1997

▼ Between June and November 1998, VAQ-139 'Cougars' completed their seventh *WestPac* in fifteen years. Three of the five months the unit spent on on deployment saw the squadron flying in the Persian Gulf supporting OSW. Reflecting the importance of the Prowler in this theatre, VAQ-139 led one-fifth of all CVW-14 missions into Iraq, despite only possessing four aircraft! The 'CAG bird' throughout the *WestPac* was ICAP II Block 89 jet BuNo 163888, whose tail markings in September 1997 are clearly shown in this close-up view. These had subtly changed by the time the deployment got underway some ten months later, with the cougar's head being altered in style to reflect the insignia worn on other jets within the unit. The marking had also been repositioned on the rudder, which was painted solid black. This particular Prowler was the 163rd of 170 production-standard EA-6Bs built for the US Navy/Marine Corps

◄ Brown-shirted plane captains from VAQ-139 apply the finishing touches to 'Cougar 620' prior to the aircraft being manned up by its crew. The jet is parked in the area immediately forward of the island known as the 'Corral', which includes both deck elevators one and two. The embarked Prowler unit will traditionally occupy three spots in this area when aboard, with the fourth jet struck down in the hangar bay undergoing routine maintenance;

'The aircraft, and its systems, are incredibly reliable, particularly when you consider the daily punishment that we subject them to during launches and recoveries. Sure, much of the electronic equipment could be made smaller and lighter, thus reducing the weight in a notoriously heavy jet, but would this new equipment stand up to the strain of carrier operations – probably not', VAQ-139 pilot Lt Cdr Scott 'Turtle' Gage told me whilst I was aboard CVN 72 in September 1997

► A constant theme that has run through all OSW deployments made by the US Navy since *Desert Storm* has been the necessity for EA-6Bs to be on station in 'the box' when other Coalition aircraft are enforcing the no-fly zone. Such mission doctrine has resulted in high workloads for both the men and machinery of the embarked Prowler unit in-theatre at the time. Between December 1998 and April 1999, the primary EW unit was VAQ-135 'Black Ravens', which saw much action supporting not only fellow CVW-11 aircraft, but also USAF and RAF jets as well;

'We support every Allied event that goes into "the box". We are an asset that has to be in "the 'box", or else the mission doesn't happen – Coalition aircraft simply move back south. We have to make sure that one Prowler is up on station at all times when a package is entering or leaving "the box" in order to cover any periods of vulnerability. Due to our mission designation, and the sheer number of hours spent over, or off, Iraq, I would consider that VAQ-135 is the most operational unit in CVW-11. We have certainly participated in more "box hop" strikes than any other squadron on the ship', one 'Black Raven' NFO proudly explained to me aboard CVN 70 in March 1999.

In this shot, a VFA-94 Hornet provides the 'meat' in a Prowler 'sandwich' in the 'Corral' on *Vinson*

◄ The hardening of the Coalition's resolve to enforce the no-fly zone through direct military action resulted in the implementation of Operation *Desert Fox* in December 1998. Following this three-day all-out assault, CVN 70 and CVW-11 was left to keep the pressure on the Iraqis with a series of follow-up strikes on key SAM, AAA, radar and command and control sites. In the vanguard was VAQ-135, and they soon realised that an extra jet was going to be needed if the squadron was to have any chance of keeping pace with the daily Air Tasking Orders emanating from CentCom – US Central Command, which is the unified command for all US forces in the Middle East. Help came in the form of veteran EA-6B BuNo 161775, resplendent in the markings of VAQ-209 'Star Warriors'. Normally shore-based at NAF Washington (Andrews AFB in Maryland), the jet was flown across the Atlantic by a reservist crew and 'loaned' to VAQ-135 for the duration of their time in the Persian Gulf. Although given the squadron identity of 'Blackraven 504', the Prowler retained all of its reservist details right down to the *USS JOHN F KENNEDY* titling on the fuselage. The aircraft was flown back to Maryland once CVN 70 was relieved of its OSW duties by the *Enterprise*

▲ The pilot's gaze is fixed on the plane director for bow cat two as he waits for the signal to tell him that 'Blackraven 503' (BuNo 158816) has been connected to the cat shuttle. The catapult crews hate working with the Prowler, for it is not only the loudest aircraft in the air wing when powered up just prior to launching, but it is also the least 'civilised' – its exhaust nozzles are angled in such a way that the jet blast actually lifts off chunks of anti-skid coating from the flightdeck and peppers those poor souls clustered aft of the wing trailing edge. Despite being by far the oldest Prowler in the unit (it was originally delivered in the mid-1970s as an EXpanded CAPability jet), this aircraft has been upgraded to current Lot 89 ICAP (Improved CAPability) standards. The lethality of these improvements is graphically shown by the two HARM symbols worn below the modex, this aircraft having fired two of the six missiles expended by the unit during its time in the Persian Gulf

▶ The pilot signals the 'shooter' with the traditional salute to acknowledge that he and his crew are set to ride CVN 70's waist cat three at the start of yet another OSW sortie. Following this ritual, both the four-man crew in the jet and the deck crew lined up on either side of 'Blackraven 503' will brace themselves for the launch – the former against the organ-crushing acceleration of the cat shot, and the latter against the stinging deck detritus flung up in the Prowler's wake

▶ A clutch of safety and ordnance personnel from VAQ-135 standby as the pilot and ECMO 1 complete the final cockpit checks in 'Blackraven 504', prior to releasing the brakes and taxying away from the 'Corral'. The white-shirted plane inspector squatting just aft of the nose gear will have to secure the crew's intake-mounted boarding ladder before the Prowler can be marshalled out. A pilot from VAQ-135 recounts the immediate pre-launch 'ritual' adopted by his unit on CVN 70;

'We go "feet on the deck" to our jet 45 minutes prior to launch, by which time the aircraft is fully fuelled, all systems are up and running thanks to external power, and the HARM missiles and ECM pods have been securely attached to the stores pylons. The jet is then preflighted from deck level for around 10-15 minutes, after which we climb aboard. With 30 minutes to run to launch, the Air Boss will call "starts away", and the aircraft are fired up. With everything running as it should be, you are then unchained and marshalled in a pre-ordained order to one of the ship's four catapults'

◀ Having extricated itself from the arrestor gear and had its HARM round rendered safe by red-shirted 'ordies' from the ship's company, 'Blackraven 502' (BuNo 163889) is swung left towards the yellow-shirted plane director standing in the back-ground. Once the jet has taxied into the 'Corral' and been shut down by the crew, specialist 'ordies' from VAQ-135 will ensure that *all* the stores (tanks, ECM pods and missiles) on the pylons are correctly 'pinned'. This task is undertaken by the armourers primarily because 'they do not trust us to do such things correctly', stated one of the unit's NFOs! He went on to explain that this EA-6B is configured in typical OSW fit;

'We usually fly with three ALQ-99 jamming pods and one drop tank. We like this configuration, as it allows us to carry a single missile – usually on one of the two inner wing pylons. We need the one external tank to give us the desired range. The pods are pre-program-med to counter what we consider to be the primary threat bands. In order to cover pretty well any EW emissions we might encounter in "the box", we always send two jets, configured with differently banded pods, along with every package. Power is everything, and the more power we have up there, the better we do. Also, if a jet launches and one of its pods refuses to work, the second jet will almost always be able to cover the threat band with one of its ALQ-99s'

◀ Storeless, bar two Aero 1D 300 US-gal underwing tanks, VAQ-135's 'CAG bird' (BuNo 163527) 'flies the ball' towards the deck of CVN 70 during a late-afternoon CQ period. Despite the Prowler's reputation for being a handful 'around the boat', the 'Black Ravens' flew their aircraft so well that the unit won CVW-11's prestigious Golden Tailhook trophy for CVN 70's final line period of *WestPac '98/'99*. 'Blackraven 500' wears a single HARM mission marker below its cockpit, although the firing of this round in January 1999 was not the first time that the aircraft had prosecuted a target in Iraq. Eight years earlier almost to the day, BuNo 163527 had gone into action with VAQ-141 'Shadowhawks' (wearing modex '621') from the deck of USS *Theodore Roosevelt*, the unit performing the SEAD mission for both CVW-8 and other Coalition assets during *Desert Storm*. The jet also completed numerous sorties in support of Operation *Provide Comfort*, which followed in the wake of the conflict. Back in 1991, BuNo 163527 had been one of the newest Prowlers in the fleet, having joined VAQ-141 as a Block 86 jet fresh from the Grumman assembly line in January 1990

▲ Getting in and out of a stationary Prowler takes some deft footwork and no small amount of agility, as the cockpit sits a good 15 feet off the flightdeck. This scene was repeated countless times by the crews of VAQ-135 whilst on station in the Persian Gulf, the unit logging 398 combat hours over Iraq (out of a total of 1050 for the full six-month deployment). I asked a 'Black Raven' NFO what the unit was doing when over Iraq;

'During a typical OSW mission we will spend the greatest percentage of our time on station in the eastern part of Iraq, listening out for signals being emitted by the various types of search and missile guidance radar scattered across "the box". We also communicate frequently with other airborne assets in order to find out what they are picking up as well. We will then try and isolate one particular signal, tracing it back to its point of origin. As soon as we enter the no-fly zone, we are ready to act the instant a "friendly" is engaged by a threat system. If an Allied jet is "locked up", we will start pressing everyone south whilst simultaneously attempting to isolate and neutralise the Iraqi radar. We will, of course, also be heading south, along with our HARM-equipped Hornets that rely on us for targeting information'

◄ Just like the rest of CVW-5's aircraft embarked on CV 63 for its OSW deployment in mid-1999, VAQ-136's quartet of Block 89 Prowlers looked like they had seen better days following endless weeks at sea aboard the US Navy's oldest warship. The 'senior' EA-6B within the unit (and the oldest aircraft in CVW-5) was this veteran jet, which had originally been delivered to the navy in BASCAP (BASic CAPability) configuration in late 1971. Periodically modified and upgraded throughout its 29 years of service to date, this Prowler is presently as capable as any EA-6B in the fleet thanks to its most recent reworking to ICAP II Block 89 specification

◄ The crew of 'Iron Claw 504' push forward in their seat straps in an effort to combat the massive acceleration that has just been unleashed by waist cat three. According to Hornet pilot Lt Duncan 'Dingo' Clendenin from VFA-113;

'The older conventional carriers have a shorter launch stroke, and you feel more of a push when the catapult fires. With the newer "nuke" carriers, the shot is more progressive, which means that you don't get all the acceleration right at the start of the launch – you pick up a lot of knots in the last third'.

This aircraft has a HARM round nestled between its external fuel tank and the fuselage, and 'Mace 204', attached to waist cat four, is similarly configured. Following the astounding success of JSOW in combat with CVW-11 in early 1999, HARM firings on OSW sorties have been restricted to situations requiring a reactive, rather than a pre-emptive, strike

► The main gear of 'Iron Claw 501' (BuNo 161242) compresses to absorb the shock of 55,000 lbs of descending Prowler making contact with the deck of CV 63. Like all EA-6B units venturing into the Persian Gulf in the wake of *Desert Fox*, VAQ-136 found itself fully immersed in a real 'shooting' war. With a third of the unit's aircrew experiencing their first *WestPac*, everyone got the chance to fill their logbooks with green ink (signifying combat missions), including 'nugget' NFO, Lt(jg) Todd Endicott;

'I have flown 13 OSW missions in just around two months so far. We always man up two aircraft for such a mission, and although both launch, only one will head into "the box", as the second jet acts as a spare. Occasionally, we will get airborne and then get told to return to the ship because the dust storms in southern Iraq have obscured any potential targets. If I was to have gone into "the box" every time I had manned up for such a mission then my sortie tally would be around 25 to 30 by now. When in the spare jet, you are really hoping that the primary aircraft is going to develop a fault that will allow you to fly the sortie instead. Our go/no-go criteria is quite extensive, which often means that the jets may be working fine, but because a receiver is faulty on the primary Prowler, the spare aircraft becomes the "go-bird" for the mission'

‘Iron Claw 504’ (BuNo 163891) strains against the arrestor cable, its pilot holding the throttles wide open until the jet has finally come to a stop. From this angle, the Prowler's recovery configuration is clearly exposed – wing leading edge slats extended and trailing edge flaps deployed, wingtip airbrakes fully open and the all-moving tailplane angled down as far as it will go. To successfully reach this stage in the sortie, the pilot will have relied heavily on his ECMO 1 sat alongside him;

'By sitting in the right seat you are undoubtedly in the best place to be an "armchair quarterback". Once you have been an ECMO 1 for some time, you get a good feel for what is right and what is wrong during carrier approaches. You can tell if you are overpowered, whether you are high or low and how much the pilot is struggling. A good ECMO 1 has to be able to divorce himself from becoming boresighted on the approach to land. The simple way to achieve this is to keep your scan moving at all times', Lt Cdr Scott 'McP' McPherson explained to me aboard CVN 72 in September 1997

AEW AND COD

▶ The master of 'techno-fiction', Tom Clancy, succinctly described the role of the Northrop Grumman E-2 Hawkeye in his excellent 1999 factual volume, *Carrier*;

'Put a sensor of sufficient resolution high enough, and you will see enemy forces before they can harm you. This is the guiding principal behind most early warning systems, from reconnaissance satellite to Unmanned Aerial Vehicles (UAVs). For naval leaders, there is no more important "high ground" than that occupied by Airborne Early Warning (AEW)'.

The squadron that has occupied the 'high ground' for CVW-14 since its formation in April 1967 is VAW-113, known as the 'Black Eagles'. When the air wing met up for it first at sea period on CVN 72 in September 1997, the unit embarked three out of its usual complement of four Hawkeyes. 'Black Eagle 600' (BuNo 164111) was amongst this trio, the aircraft being devoid of any distinguishing unit markings due to its recent arrival from VAW-112 'Golden Hawks'. Its stay with VAW-113 was to be a very brief one, however, for this new-build Group II Hawkeye (note the Roman 'II' below the '+' symbol on nose) had been returned to its former owners prior to the 'Black Eagles' deploying on their *WestPac* in June 1998

▲ Parked in the 'Hummer Hole' – the traditional resting place for E-2s between sorties – alongside an S-3B from VS-35, 'Black Eagle 603 (BuNo 164492) displays VAW-113's muted squadron emblem and a more prominent Roman II marking on its nose. This aircraft was one of 36 new-production Group II E-2Cs to join the fleet between 1992 and 1994, this version being the first to make use of the Lockheed Martin AN/APS-145 ARPS (Advanced Radar Processing System) in place of the venerable APS-139 radar fitted into Group I Hawkeyes. Aside from the radar, Group II aircraft also utilise the superior L-304 computer processing system, which collates and processes information from the AN/ALR-73 Passive Detection System, IFF (Identification Friend or Foe) and ASN-92/ASN-50 Navigation Suite (incorporating GPS). This information is then displayed on the three individual consoles fitted 'in the back' for the trio of NFO controllers. The combination of the ARPS and L-304 mean that a Group II E-2C can simultaneously track up to 2000 targets in some six million cubic miles of airspace and 150,000 square miles of territory!

▲ Having been 'waved off' due to the deck still being fouled from the previous recovery, 'Wallbanger 600' (BuNo 164483) flies over CVN 70 at barely 200 ft in 'down and dirty' configuration. Like the Prowler, the Hawkeye is one of the more interesting naval types 'around the boat', as VAW-113's Lt Tom 'Heavy G' Gelker explained to me during my time aboard CVN 72 in September 1997;

'The E-2 is a challenging aircraft to bring back aboard the ship due to its size and the torque factor created by its non-counter rotating props. This challenge is the principal reason why I chose E-2s after completing flight school. Anyone can fly a fast jet back aboard a ship, thanks to the abundance of power on offer and its small physical size, which goes a long way to negating any real line-up problems. Although the approach speed for the E-2 is much slower than for any jet type, the aeroplane is moving in so many different directions at once with every power correction that it requires real skill as a pilot to recover the aircraft safely at sea'

▼ After flying the pattern once more, the pilot of 'Wallbanger 600' completes the recovery cycle by taking a four-wire trap back onto the ship. The E-2 is always the first aircraft to launch at the start of a cycle, or OSW mission, and then the last back aboard. Indeed, thanks to its frugal Allison T56-A-427 turboshaft engines, the Hawkeye usually stays aloft for four to five hours. In that time it could handle up to three separate packages of carrier aircraft if the air wing is conducting peacetime cyclic ops, or two staggered packages on a typical OSW mission. Following *Desert Fox*, the mission profile for the embarked airborne early warning squadron changed dramatically, as a seasoned NFO from VAW-117 pointed out to me aboard CVN 70 in March 1999;

'On past deployments, whilst providing coverage for patrols, we would often fly missions that would last up to 12 hours straight. However, because of the actual combat missions we are presently supporting, we fly in and out with the strike package on task, which has meant that our sorties have been appreciably shorter in duration. The adrenaline rush experienced when controlling aircraft that are going in over the coast and dropping bombs for real is incredible. We've told our junior guys that they really have to savour this, because it doesn't happen too regularly during your career. Previous *WestPacs* were often extremely boring due to the lack of action in "the box". If you did pick up an Iraqi aerial contact on radar, it came as a complete surprise. However, on this cruise contacts have been detected on numerous sorties'

▲ 'Wallbanger 603' (BuNo 164108) was the oldest of the quartet of E-2s assigned to VAW-117 during *WestPac '98/99*, this aircraft actually having the distinction of being the first Group II Hawkeye built by Grumman. It was delivered to the fleet in mid-1992, and was assigned to its current unit in 1994. VAW-117 is presently unique in being the only E-2 squadron in the fleet to apply the last digit in the aircraft's modex between the cockpit roof windows (which double as ditching hatches)

◀ VAW-117's 'CAG bird' was no stranger to either the deck of CVN 70 or the Persian Gulf, having previously served with VAW-113 during CVW-14's 1994 *WestPac*. Due to the extremely high number of missions being flown into 'the box', the command and control of coalition air assets is shared between the quartet of E-2s embarked on the duty carrier and land-based USAF (and occasionally RAF and Royal Saudi Air Force) E-3s;

'When operating off the coast of Iraq, we work closely with the USAF E-3 that is also performing the command and control mission in the area, maintaining a common datalink with our counterparts in the other aircraft. We are in constant communication with them on all of our missions, and between us, we set up contracts to decide who is going to provide major control for which portions of "the box". We would happily take on more of the E-3's load as well, for I believe that our Group II E-2Cs are so mission-capable that we are being under-utilised. For example, we typically schedule five missions a day, and only two of these are dedicated to OSW. The crews flying the non-OSW sorties on the schedule often feel "ripped off" that they have not got to participate in an operational mission. The latter sorties really are the "carrots on the stick" out here', a pilot from VAW-117 explained to me

▲ When it comes to aircraft with 'presence' out on the flightdeck, the Hawkeye is big enough to grab everybody's attention, especially when on 'finals' to the ship.

'At the point when the tailhook on the E-2 engages the wire, its 80 ft 8 in wingspan gives us exactly five feet of clearance on either side from the aircraft parked near the stern of the carrier. Accurate line up is therefore critically important for me when I am coming down on my approach, for if I am out by as little as five feet either wingtip will be clipping stationary aircraft. Indeed, during training at the FRS, we are taught that checking our line up is second only to watching the "meatball" during our scan on approach to the ship. Monitoring the angle of attack is third in our list of priorities,' stated E-2 pilot Lt Tom 'Heavy G' Gelker of VAW-113.

Standing on the safe side of the all-important foul deck line, which borders the angled landing area up on the carrier's 'roof', a clutch of deckcrewmen study the progress of 'Liberty 601' (BuNo 165294) as its pilot 'flies the ball' onto CV 63

◄ 'Liberty 601' strains on the arrestor wire, its co-pilot keeping a watchful eye on the blue-shirted aircraft handler (out of shot) away to the aircraft's right. Once the tailhook has released the cable, the deckcrewman will inform them by hand signals that the aircraft is free to taxy away towards the bow of the ship. Just as the '00' aircraft (or '10' in the Seahawk unit) within any embarked squadron is assigned to the CAG, so the '01' machine bears the name of the unit's CO. In VAW-115's case, their CO during *WestPac '99* was CV 63's 'unofficial mayor', Cdr Matt 'Gucci' Klunder, who had been XO during the unit's OSW deployment aboard USS *Independence* (CV 62) in 1998

▶ A key 'player' in CVW-5's ability to project power over southern Iraq, VAW-115 was heavily involved in supporting OSW missions right from the start. And being a part of the FDNF air wing, the 'Liberty Bells' sailed into the Persian Gulf well prepared to take over the naval AEW tasking from VAW-126, embarked with CVW-3 on the *Enterprise*;

'Prior to arriving in the Gulf, we had participated in Exercise *Tandem Thrust*, off Guam. This had lasted for four weeks, and in that time we had flown a record 400 hours in support of the exercise. We were then told that our presence was required on OSW, which meant that the only "rest period" the squadron got after a month of intensive flying was the nine days it took the carrier to transit across the Indian Ocean to the Persian Gulf! We slotted straight into the OSW mission once we arrived in-theatre, and it felt as if we had not "skipped a beat" since we were out here in early 1998 aboard USS *Independence*. *Tandem Thrust* stood us in good stead for the OSW mission, as the serials that we were flying with the Aussies, Canadians and other US military assets during the exercise were not too dissimilar to the sorties that we are now undertaking for real here', explained Cdr Klunder

▲ Hand signals are usually the only way that the aircrew and the deckcrew can communicate with each other once the air boss has signalled 'starts away'. Having successfully fired up both T56s, the pilot confirms his satisfaction with the mechanical state of his E-2 to the aircraft's plane captain through a traditional 'thumb's up' gesture, which is in turn reciprocated from deck level. Although VAW-115 had to cope with a heavy work-load during WestPac '99, its cause was greatly added by the quartet of new-build, or upgraded, Group II E-2Cs that had been taken on strength in late 1998. Having struggled through its previous WestPac with some of the oldest Group 0 aircraft in frontline service, VAW-115's mission capabilities were drastically improved following the arrival in Japan of two brand new aircraft fresh from Northrop Grumman (BuNos 165294 and 165295), along with a pair of Group I upgrades (BuNos 163698 and 164107) acquired from CVW-9's VAW-112

▲ In an effort to foster *esprit de corps* amongst the maintenance personnel stuck on the boat for weeks on end fixing aircraft in the oppressive heat of the Persian Gulf in high summer, some units within CVW-5 encouraged nicknames to be applied to their aircraft. VAW-115 was one such squadron;

'We have *Radar Love*, inspired by the rotating dome, *"HEAVY METAL"*, due to the fact that she has given us some maintenance problems on cruise, *BIG DADDY*, because he is always "cooking" and never lets us down, and finally *BATTLE HUMMER*, whose name reflects the noise made by the E-2's twin turbo-prop engines', Cdr Klunder proudly explained to me. Seen during a period of full serviceability, *"HEAVY METAL"* (BuNo 164107) taxies away from the 'Hummer Hole' on CV 63

◀ 'Liberty 600' (BuNo 165295) is guided towards the bow cats at the start of a launch cycle. Getting an aircraft of this size into the right place at the right time takes some organising, and VAW-113's Lt(jg) Tom 'Heavy G' Gelker ran through what he had to do as a pilot in order to get his Hawkeye safely onto the cat;

'The visibility out of the E-2 on the deck is pretty poor, so as soon as you strap in, the pilot takes responsibility for everything on the left hand side of the aircraft and the co-pilot covers the right. Due to the tight working environment of the carrier deck, and the large size of the E-2, you have to strictly obey the instructions of your yellow-shirt. The pilot keeps his eyes fixed on the deckcrewman at all times, with his left hand on the nosewheel steering and his right hand on the power levers, carefully manoeuvring the aircraft onto the catapult. This takes up all of his time, leaving him unable to deal with the take-off checklist. This is where the co-pilot becomes essential, for he will be both reading the checklist and carrying out the responses. He will be squaring the aircraft away for take-off, and if he has performed his job correctly, by the time the E-2 is connected to the cat, all the pilot will have to do prior to the launch is scan his instruments to ensure that all systems are functioning properly'

◀ The most unglamorous aircraft type on the flightdeck, the humble C-2 Greyhound nevertheless performs a vital job for both the air wing and the ship's company, providing the 'air bridge' between the CV/CVN and shore bases. Boasting the same wingspan as the E-2, the C-2 requires a similar level of precision handling from the pilot when on short finals;

'As with the Hawkeye, the Greyhound is the most difficult aircraft to bring aboard the carrier because of its 80-ft 7-in wingspan, non-counter rotating props and 125-knot approach speed. We don't have a HUD, auto-throttle or stability augmentation in the approach configuration. There's no difference between the old A-1 Spads coming aboard and a C-2

or E-2, except that we have to land on the centreline. Whilst a Hornet can land safely in the box left or right of the centreline, the C-2/E-2 must go down the middle. We fly the aircraft into the wires, feet working the rudders continuously even after touch down, seeking the exact centre of the landing area', recounted Capt D T 'Tex' Keuhlen, Commander AEW Wing Atlantic, to *Wings of Gold* magazine in 1999.

The pilot of VRC-30 Det 2's 'Password 37' (BuNo 162171) is seen 'working the ball' as he closes on CVN 70 for a dusk recovery in March 1999

◀ The US Navy presently has just two fleet-going Carrier Onboard Delivery (COD) squadrons, with all training requirements for the C-2 force being undertaken by the combined E-2/C-2-equipped VAW-120 at NAS Norfolk. Typically, east coast-based VRC-40 'Rawhides' will support the AirLant carriers when at sea, and VRC-30 'Providers' will perform a similar role for the AirPac CV/CVNs. The fleet logistic support units each control a fleet of around 15 Greyhounds apiece, with the training flight within VAW-120 having a further five C-2s on strength. The last new-build COD was delivered to the navy in 1989, and in recent years the Greyhound fleet has begun to show its age with bouts of unreliability hitting the fleet. For example, during CVN 70's *WestPac '98/99* deployment VRC-30 Det 2 suffered a series of engine failures that kept both its Greyhounds grounded for days on end. Indeed, things got so bad at one point that the carrier had to rely on the two utility-configured MH-53E Sea Dragons operated by the Bahrain-based HC-4 det for its sole COD support. Unserviceable, and awaiting attention from Det 2's hard-working maintenance team, 'Password 37' sits silently in the 'Junk Yard' behind CVN 70's island and antenna mast

No such technical maladies afflicted Det 5 aboard CV 63 during CVW-5's *WestPac*, its C-2As (BuNos' 162147 and 162164) performing all the support missions asked of them during the carrier's 91 days on the line in the Persian Gulf. 'Password 430' taxies forward towards the bow cats at the start of yet another flight, the COD usually being the first aircraft to depart during a typical launch cycle. Whilst in the Persian Gulf, the C-2s will be flying a near-daily programme of short 35- to 50-minute shuttle missions between the navy's facility at Bahrain International Airport and the duty carrier. Cargoes can range from sailors (up to a total of 28) joining/departing the ship, or VIPs embarking for a brief visit, to 10,000 lbs of mail or a solitary replacement engine for perhaps a Tomcat or Hornet. Overall, during a typical six-month-long *WestPac*, the two-aircraft det will move over 2500 people and 750,000 lbs of cargo

The Assistant Plane Director for bow cat one gives the pilot of 'Password 431' the signal to apply the brakes, as the C-2 is now in the correct position to facilitate attachment to the launch shuttle. When assigned to an air wing for the duration of the deployment, the embarked Greyhounds will adopt the former's two-letter tailcode, which in CVW-5's case is 'NF'. Despite the type's rather chequered immediate past in respect to its serviceability, the Greyhound is always the most immaculate aircraft to be seen on any carrier deck. This may have something to do with the fact that the C-2 is often the first fleet-capable aircraft VIPs get to see 'in the flesh', and the US Navy is always keen to create a positive impression amongst it visitors. 'Password 431' was no exception to this rule, boasting a highly polished glossy grey and white finish, black radome and fully intact VRC-30 and CVW-5 25th anniversary decals

'Launch the COD!' 'Password 430' climbs away from the bow of CV 63, the pilot having already selected gear retraction – note the angle of the wheel on the port gear leg. The small protuberance below the rear loading ramp is a retractable tail bumper, which is extended for both launches and recoveries. The full colour marking on the outer fins of this particular aircraft denoted that it was the 'CAG bird' for VRC-30, the unit having just one of its fifteen C-2s so decorated

SEAHAWKS

▶ During the Cold War, one of the US Navy's primary missions was anti-submarine warfare (ASW), with the purpose-built S-3 Viking being the ultimate carrier-based platform for the prosecution of this specialist tasking. Following the 'melt-down' of the Soviet Union in the early 1990s, and the subsequent drastic reduction in the threat posed to the carrier battle group by communist submarines, the ASW mission has been effectively passed from the east and west coast Sea Control Wings (to which the S-3s are assigned) to the Helicopter Anti-submarine Wings. Some ten fleet-going units are split evenly between the two wings, with four AirPac squadrons (and a fifth forward-deployed to NAF Atsugi, Japan) based at NAS North Island, in California, and five AirLant squadrons assigned to NAS Jacksonville, in Florida. They are all equipped with variants of the Sikorsky Seahawk helicopter, the squadrons typically operating a mix of four or five ASW-equipped SH-60Fs (unofficially dubbed 'Ocean Hawks' or 'CV Helos') and two or three HH-60Hs (known to crews as 'Rescue Hawks'). CVW-14's dedicated ASW unit is HS-4 'Black Knights', and in September 1997 this SH-60F (BuNo 164449) was one of five Seahawks flown out to CVN 72 from NAS North Island for the air wing's first carrier work-ups aboard their then new home

▶ The pilot of 'Blacknight 612' pulls up and breaks away from the camera, revealing both the circular housing for the Bendix Oceanics AN/ASQ-13F dipping sonar (positioned immediately below the fuselage window) and the vertical sonobuoy launch tubes (centrally placed in line with the forward sponsons). Like the remaining squadrons embarked on CVN 72 during the September 1997 TSTA-II/-III period, HS-4 was conducting its own programme of unit-level work-ups within CVW-14, as Lt Cdr Tom 'Nose' Nosenzo explained to me;

'Every pilot, no matter what their rank, requires six day deck landings to become carrier qualified for daylight operations. The same number is deemed necessary to become night qualified, and one of these must be a night approach through the CCA (Carrier-Controlled Approach) to a holding position alongside the ship. When conducting work-ups with new crews, we try and pair up junior guys with senior pilots, and second tour pilots with each other so that everyone gets a good range of flying experience in the shortest possible time. We often struggle to get our pilots carrier deck qualified during work-ups simply because the air wing finds it hard to work our rotary-winged require-ments into its predominantly fixed-wing flying programme. Once the last fixed-wing aircraft have recovered, everybody wants to shut the deck down for the day, leaving us with little opportunity to perform our dedicated landing practice'

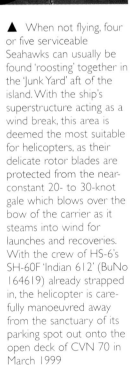

▲ When not flying, four or five serviceable Seahawks can usually be found 'roosting' together in the 'Junk Yard' aft of the island. With the ship's superstructure acting as a wind break, this area is deemed the most suitable for helicopters, as their delicate rotor blades are protected from the near-constant 20- to 30-knot gale which blows over the bow of the carrier as it steams into wind for launches and recoveries. With the crew of HS-6's SH-60F 'Indian 612' (BuNo 164619) already strapped in, the helicopter is carefully manoeuvred away from the sanctuary of its parking spot out onto the open deck of CVN 70 in March 1999

◀ HS-6's 'CAG bird' – or 'Indian Chief' – aboard CVN 70 in 1998-99 was BuNo 164082, which was issued to the unit just prior to CVW-11 deploying on cruise following a three-year spell with the Seahawk FRS, HS-10 'Taskmasters'. One of the oldest SH-60Fs in the fleet, this machine had been delivered from Sikorsky to HS-2 'Golden Falcons' in the spring of 1990, and subsequently took part in the 'CV Helo's' first operational carrier deployment, with CVW-9 aboard the *Nimitz*, a year later. A veteran of several *WestPacs*, the helicopter saw extensive use whilst in the Persian Gulf with HS-6 in 'Truck' configuration – stripped of the dipping sonar equipment and various other internal ASW-oriented 'boxes'. When 'gutted out', the SH-60F is the ideal platform for Maritime Interception Operations (MIO), which will see a Seahawk operating in conjunction with surface ships (destroyers and frigates) enforcing the blockade on Iraqi ports in the northern extremes of the Persian Gulf. Flying from the *Arleigh Burke*-class destroyer USS *Fitzgerald* (DDG 62) and the *Oliver Hazard Perry*-class frigate USS *Klakring* (FFG 42), Seahawks from HS-6 were involved in MIO between 28 February and 5 March. The eagle-eyed amongst you will have spotted Venice Beach-based American aviation photographer David Peters training his Nikon camera out the open cabin door at me, and I in turn was doing the self-same thing back at him!

◀ Although the bulk of carrier-based Seahawks are F-models, in the Persian Gulf the most useful variant is the utility-configured HH-60H. Lt Cdr Tom 'Nose' Nosenzo again;

'When performing the OSW mission, typically the "Foxtrots" will remain stripped for the whole time the carrier is on station, for there is no real ASW threat in the region. Indeed, the only navy taking submarines into these waters is ours. With high temperatures being experienced pretty well all year round, to lose the 575 lbs of weight associated with the ASW equipment helps boost the helicopter's performance'.

No such 'gutting out' was required for this particular helicopter, for 'Indian 614' (BuNo 165113) was one of three dedicated H-models embarked aboard CVN 70 for *WestPac '98/99*. A variety of specialist equipment unique to the H-model can be seen in this view, including the angled wirestrike protection system 'spike' just forward of the rotor hub, the raised platform for the Sanders AN/ALQ-144 infra-red jammer aft of the hub, Hover Infra-Red Suppressor System (HIRSS) fairings over both exhausts, and AN/ALE-39 chaff/flare dispensers in mid-fuselage housings

► The 'bread and butter' mission for any embarked Seahawk unit aboard a CV/CVN is plane guard, for NATOPS regulations state that a helicopter must be airborne at all times during launches and recoveries. A second helicopter is also held at readiness back on the flightdeck throughout this period.

'You can perform the plane guard mission in either the "Foxtrot" or "Hotel" model helicopter, although there is a lot more room in the latter. If you get a multi-seat aircraft go in and all the crew punch out, but are injured in the process, you can only really fit one person in the back of an SH-60F. We often fly with the F-models in "Truck" configuration for that very reason, and with the ASW equipment being of modular design, it takes around two to three hours to strip the aircraft out, and around four hours to put it all back in again', explained HS-4's Lt Cdr Tom 'Nose' Nosenzo.

Having covered the launch of the mid-morning OSW strike package, 'Indian 610' cruises past the bow of CVN 70 whilst awaiting the return of the first wave of the day

▼ Aside from undertaking the ASW and plane guard missions, HS-6 also performed the fleet logistics role for the carrier battle group (CVBG) whilst on the line in support of OSW. CVN 70's battle group (Carrier Group Three) during *WestPac '98/99* consisted of two Aegis cruisers, two destroyers, a frigate, two submarines and an oiler/ammunition vessel. One of the two *Ticonderoga*-class cruisers within CARGRU-3 was USS *Princeton* (CG 59), which was employed primarily to screen CVBGs with its legendary Aegis Anti-Air Warfare radar system. Although possessing the best anti-air missile system presently in service with any navy, the 27-strong *Ticonderoga* class guided-missile cruisers are incredibly versatile ships, boasting a combat-proven land-attack/strike capability centred around the Raytheon BGM-109 Tomahawk cruise missile. The aft battery of the Vertical Launch System (VLS) for CG 59's Tomahawks can be seen stepped down from the modest flightdeck recently vacated by 'Indian 610'. The San Diego-based *Princeton* observed two memorable dates in its brief history during its OSW patrol in 1998-99 – the vessel had been commissioned on 11 February 1989, and struck an Iraqi bottom-laid influence mine (which detonated a second device) on 18 February 1991 whilst participating in *Desert Storm*. Coincidentally, HS-6 was originally formed in 1956 to serve aboard the *Essex*-class amphibious assault carrier USS *Princeton* (LPH 5)

▶ Having completed yet another day's flying, 'Indian 614' has had its rotors firmly pinned back and tail assembly folded into its stowed position, prior to being towed across the flightdeck to the 'Junk Yard'. Combat Search And Rescue (C-SAR) is another important tasking adopted by the various HELANTISUBRONs within the Helicopter Anti-submarine Wings following the advent of the HH-60H.

'I only flew a limited number of C-SAR sorties with the Sea King, for the navy then had dedicated reserve-manned C-SAR units. This all changed with the arrival of Seahawks on carriers, and we went from having four mission commanders who had a C-SAR "qual" during the SH-3 days, to the present situation where we have around ten per unit. Seven of these pilots are department heads and the CO and XO, whilst the remaining three will be first tour guys who have got their "quals" whilst with the unit', HS-4's Lt Cdr Tom 'Nose' Nosenzo told me in September 1997.

HS-6 enjoyed a concentrated period of 'Combat-SAR' flying between 2 January and 20 February 1999 when a detachment of two HH-60Hs and two crews were sent to Camp Doha, in Kuwait, to stand C-SAR alert in support of OSW missions over southern Iraq

▶ The sole forward-deployed Seahawk unit is HS-14 'Chargers', whose five SH-60Fs and two HH-60Hs have called NAF Atsugi home since September 1994 following the disestablishment of Sea King-equipped HS-12 'Wyverns'. A part of the CVW-2/*Ranger* combination from the time of the unit's establishment in 1984 through to the decommissioning of CV 61 in 1993, HS-14 transitioned from venerable SH-3H Sea Kings to a mix of new SH-60Fs and HH-60Hs prior to its assignment to CVW-5. Painted in typically drab TPS greys, 'Lightning 614' slowly descends towards the deck of CV 63 in June 1999. Below the helicopter can be seen the crucially important Optical Landing System (OLS), or 'meat-ball' as it is irreverently known to all naval aviators

▲ In comparison with the remaining six Seahawks assigned to HS-14, 'Lightning 610' (BuNo 164797) was a 'riot of colour' during CV 63's *WestPac '99*, befitting its status as the 'CAG bird'. Not satisfied with simply applying a large coloured decal of the squadron's badge and a blue fuselage modex, HS-14 adorned the SH-60F in the markings seen here prior to embarking on deployment in March 1999. This helicopter has served exclusively with the 'Chargers' since its delivery to the navy in 1993, and for much of the time it has worn variations on the coloured CAG marking theme. Prior to this scheme being adopted, HS-14 had restricted itself to a series of modest-sized rainbow-coloured chevrons applied vertically along the leading edge of 'Lightning 610's' tail rotor pylon. Full-colour 'star & bars' and multi-coloured ship/air wing titling on the fairing immediately above the cockpit completed its previous CAG decoration

SCOUTS AND SHADOWS

▶ It is one of post-Cold War naval aviation's greatest ironies that the previously mission-specific Lockheed S-3 Viking has become arguably the air wing's greatest 'all-rounder'. And this evolution from sub-hunter to sea controller, surface reconnaissance platform and the air wing's sole aerial tanking asset has made the venerable jet one of the most mission-critical aircraft to be found on the deck of a CV/CVN today. With the advent of these extra missions, and the virtual abandonment of its ASW tasking, the Viking community now finds itself busier than at any stage in the jet's 25-year history with the fleet. The newest unit within either of the two Sea Control Wings (five fleet-going AirLant squadrons are based at NAS Jacksonville, with a similar number at NAS North Island assigned to AirPac) is VS-35 'Blue Wolves', which was re-established as an S-3 unit in April 1991. As an ASW squadron originally dises-tablished in 1973 following almost 20 years of front-line service in S2F Trackers, VS-35 had tried twice before to rejoin the fleet with Vikings, and on both occasions fallen foul of either operational constraints (in 1977) or budgetary cuts (in 1988). Assigned to CVW-14 following its latest reincar-nation, VS-35 served with the air wing aboard CVN 70 until it moved to CVN 72 in 1997. The unit's 'CAG bird' (BuNo 159745) is seen aboard *Lincoln* in September 1997

▲ Like the remaining units within CVW-14, VS-35 was conducting cyclic ops aboard CVN 72 during its brief at-sea period with the vessel, having embarked six of its eight S-3Bs from its NAS North Island home. Amongst the numerous 'nugget' pilots tackling his first 'CQ' with a frontline unit was Lt(jg) Paul 'Catfish' Schaller, who explained to me what it was like flying a Viking 'around the boat';

'When compared with other jet types in the air wing, the S-3 is amongst the easiest to land back aboard thanks to its slow-speed handling, but like any other aircraft, it still has its peculiarities and quirks. For example, its wing is straight at the trailing edge, making it gust responsive. This wind sensitivity is accentuated by the aircraft's slow approach speed. Whereas a Hornet or Tomcat can simply zip through the "burble" of disturbed air trailing in the carrier's wake at around 135 to 145 knots, we really feel the effect of it as we have to push through at speeds some 20 to 25 knots slower.'

Freshly resprayed just prior to embarkation, 'Blue Wolf 703' (BuNo 160582) was the youngest of the six S-3Bs aboard *Lincoln* in September 1997. A *Desert Shield* veteran with VS-37 (and, ironically, CVW-14) aboard the *Independence* in 1990-91, this aircraft has completed at least six *WestPacs* since being delivered to the navy in 1978. These include four cruises with VS-29 (three on CVN 70 in 1983, 1985 and 1986, and one aboard CVN 72 in 1993) and two with VS-37 (CV 64 in 1989 and CV 62 in 1990-91)

◀ Aside from the 'vanilla' ASW/Sea Control Viking, the navy has also operated two other specialised versions of the S-3 which are now no longer in fleet service. Four aircraft were designated US-3A CODs following the removal of all their ASW-related equipment, whilst two more were also partially reconfigured for the fleet logistics role, although they retained the S-3A designation. These jets served with VRC-50 in support of carriers on *WestPac* from 1977 through until their wholesale retirement in 1994. The second variant to make it onto the flightdeck in an operational capacity was the ES-3A Shadow. Developed in the early 1990s as a Tactical Airborne Signal Exploitation System aircraft to undertake the electronic intelligence (ELINT) and signals intelligence (SIGINT) roles previously performed by the EA-3B Skywarrior, 16 Shadows were remanufactured using surplus S-3As. Delivered to VQ-5 at NAS Agana, Guam, and VQ-6 at NAS Cecil Field, Florida, the Shadows undertook their first operational deployments in 1993. Moving to NAS North Island (VQ-5) and NAS Jacksonville (VQ-6), both units split their modest force into four detachments of two aircraft apiece, and these would accompany air wings on six-month deployments across the globe. Part of VQ-5's Det Bravo, this Shadow (BuNo 1588623) was the sole aircraft sent out to CVN 72 for CVW-14's TSTA-II/-III period in September 1997

▲ The Shadows remained a key part of the air wing until retired – some senior officers believe prematurely – in mid-1999. The removal of the aircraft from the fleet followed the navy's official announcement in June 1998 that it would not fund the upgrade required to make the modest fleet compatible with the Joint Airborne SIGINT Structure (JASA) standard. The latter is presently being developed to allow all USAF, US Navy and US Army ELINT/SIGINT airborne assets to communicate with each other when on station. Instead, air wings must now rely on the two-dozen land-based EP-3Es which have been tasked with supporting forward-deployed CV/CVNs from airfields in the Middle East, Europe and the Far East. The last operational cruises undertaken by the ES-3A came to an end on 6 May 1999 when VQ-5's Det Bravo departed CVN 70 for NAS North Island and VQ-6's Det Alpha launched from CVN 65 and flew to NAS Jacksonville. Two months earlier, I was fortunate enough to photograph Det Bravo in action aboard *Carl Vinson*, supporting CVW-11's commitment to OSW. In a sight now consigned to history, 'Seashadow 723' (BuNo 159415') taxies aft along with a S-3B from VS-29

▲ The ES-3Bs were highly valued by CentCom during CVN 70's period on the line in the Persian Gulf, being continually tasked.

'All of our missions once here in the Gulf have been in support of OSW. We will fly off independently of a strike package, patrolling along the Iraqi coast moni- toring the EW traffic that their presence throws up. When we go up north, we fly on a specifically desig- nated track. We initially stay on station for around 30 to 45 minutes to feel the situation out and get together as much information on the EW traffic as possible. We

launch ahead of the "strikers" partly because the Air Boss wants to make sure that he can get us off the deck! We arrive on station well ahead of the package, and stick around for about an hour after they have egressed from "the box" so as to see what comms traffic they have stirred up in their wake, before heading home', Det Bravo pilot, Lt Dan 'Diamond' Ogden, related to me. Dan's assigned aircraft (BuNo 158862) heads a line up of Vikings parked in the 'Corral', this ES-3A having been embarked on CVN 70 in March 1999 during the carrier's *WestPac*

▲ The domed fairing for the spinning OE-320 ELINT direction-finding antennas is visible forward of the folded wings in this view of a Det Bravo ES-3A seen 'at rest' in the 'Hummer Hole'. The AN/ALR-76 ESM (Electronic Surveillance Measures) wingtip antennas fitted to the Shadow were identical to those used by the S-3B, although the 'towel rail' ALD-9 Air Loop HF-DF (High Frequency-Direction Finding) antennae inboard of the pods were unique to the ES-3A. The pilot of the Shadow was also the Electronic Warfare Aircraft Commander (EWAC), and two his right was sat the EW Combat Co-ordinator (EWCC). The latter's workstation differed substantially from the co-pilot's cockpit in a standard S-3B, as all the 'safety of flight' equipment (control column, throttle and rudder pedals) had been removed, leaving only rudimentary flight instrumentation

▲ Despite possessing just two aircraft, three complete crews and 43 maintenance personnel, VQ-5 Det Bravo completed more than 280 flight hours directly in support of coalition assets operating in 'the box'.

'In December we completed a 100 per cent sortie rate, which is a hell of a thing for any unit, let alone a two-aircraft det that effectively has no spares source to call on. This achievement is all the more impressive when you consider that our jets have flown a third more hours than any other aircraft in the air wing over the same period. Seen as a high value asset, when the ES-3A is "down" on the flightdeck due to technical problems, it attracts serious attention from the CAG on up. It therefore does our buddies in the larger S-3 unit some good to help us out, and keep the jets flying. One of the great ironies of this final *WestPac* deployment for the ES-3A is that the jet has flown sustained combat missions for the first time, Det Bravo proving the platform's ability right on the eve of its retirement', lamented EWCC, Lt Amy 'Princess' Kingston

▲ A trio of well-worn S-3Bs from VS-29 'Screaming Dragonfires' sit alongside four equally weathered Hornets from VFA-94 and VFA-97 on CVN 70. The notoriously 'short-legged' F/A-18 was the former unit's principal customer during *WestPac '98/99*, the strike-fighters utilising the Viking's tanking capabilities on virtually every sortie. Much to the chagrin of many junior S-3 pilots, aerial refuelling has become the primary tasking for the Sea Control community since the KA-6D Intruder was retired in 1996. VS-35's Operations Officer, Lt Cdr Colin Chaffee, had the

following to say about the Viking's crucial support mission;

'Currently, 60 to 70 per cent of the S-3B sorties flown from the carrier involve the transfer of needed fuel to other platforms, and nearly every flight will include a "package check" to ensure that the buddy store is operational in the event that it is needed. However, this still encompasses only 14-16 per cent of the total deployed flight time. The majority of these missions will be dual-tasked. The aircraft will fill the tanking role following take-off, and once the previous event's recovery is complete, the crew will depart the tanker pattern to provide surface surveillance, ASW or other mission services to a warfare commander. Often, after a mission, the S-3 will return to the overhead above the carrier a few minutes early to fulfil the recovery tanker role, and provide a "package check" for the oncoming tanker. Due to the characteristics of the aircraft in today's air wing, you can't escape the tanking mission, but you can ensure that the aircraft are employed intelligently while meeting those tanking requirements'

▶ VS-29's 'CAG bird' (BuNo 159387) is seen on that rare occasion when devoid of the underwing combination of the A/A42R-1 refuelling store on the port pylon and an Aero-1D 300-US gal fuel tank to starboard. Instead, 'Dragonfire 700' has been uploaded with three Mk 7 dispensers per triple ejector rack, each of these being filled with CBU-99 bomblets. This configuration is typical for a Viking tasked with carrying out an Armed Surface Reconnaissance (ASR) of the Northern Arabian Gulf (NAG). This sea control mission is tasked by CentCom every single day, and whilst one aircraft is airborne flying the patrol, a second Viking with an identical ordnance load-out will be sat on the deck of the carrier ready to assist the primary aircraft should it encounter Iraqi fast patrol boats acting aggressively in international waters. A veteran of *Desert Shield* with VS-31 aboard USS *Dwight D Eisenhower* (CVN 69), this particular Viking served with numerous NAS Cecil Field-based units prior to joining VS-33 at NAS North Island in the early 1990s. It subsequently became VS-29's 'CAG bird' in 1997

▲ 'Dragonfire 701' (BuNo 160596) edges towards the shuttle for waist cat three, the hook-up crew giving the plane director the signal to instruct the pilot to keep the jet moving slowly forward. On a typical OSW mission, two S-3s are launched off at the start of the cycle to perform the role of duty tankers for the strike package, and VS-29 excelled itself in this role as soon as CVN 70 arrived in-theatre. Indeed, CVW-11's first OSW mission took the form of the last strike of *Desert Fox*, and due to the unavailability of USAF tankers, VS-29's S-3Bs became the sole source of inflight refuelling for the 20 aircraft sent 300 miles into Iraq at night to hit a variety of targets. This duly made the mission an all-navy affair. During CVN 70's period on the line, the eight S-3Bs assigned to the 'Screaming Dragonfires' offloaded 1.6 million pounds of fuel to CVW-11 aircraft

▲ Despite VS-29's outstanding 97 per cent sortie completion rate during its most recent *WestPac*, the Sea Control squadrons are all suffering from the unreliability associated with operating old aircraft. A two-tour OSW veteran, Lt Dan 'Stool' Kauffman of VS-35 has full experience of these problems;

'The S-3 is a good jet, but it is most definitely starting to show its age. The biggest challenges that we face don't centre around performing the mission itself, but rather keeping the aircraft serviceable to simply fly the mission. The S-3 is now prone to breaking down on a regular basis. I wouldn't say that the jets we fly are sub-standard, but they are certainly old. Unlike aircrew operating other types within the air wing, we as members of the Sea Control community have to deal far more with systems reliability issues, and how best to work around technical problems in order to still fulfil the mission brief.'

One of the oldest jets within VS-29 was 'Dragonfire 707' (BuNo 159399), which was delivered to the navy in late 1974, and more recently served with VS-33 prior to being issued to VS-29 in 1998

◀ Fuel reserves exhausted, 'Dragonfire 705' (BuNo 159409) descends over the frothy wake churned up by CVN 70 as the carrier carves its way through the still waters of the Persian Gulf. One of the last A-models converted into a Bravo, this aircraft served for many years with VS-38. It completed a string of three *WestPacs* with the unit as part of CVW-2 aboard the *Ranger* between 1989 and 1993, the middle one of these seeing the aircraft participate in *Desert Storm*. Following conversion, the Viking returned to VS-38 in 1996, and remained with the 'Red Griffins' until it was transferred to VS-29 upon the completion of the former unit's *WestPac '97* deployment aboard USS *Constellation* (CV 64)

▲ Of the nine S-3s aboard CV 63 in 1999, eight carried the familiar Viking head and lightning bolt emblem traditionally associated with VS-21, whilst the ninth featured this stunning marking derived from the unit's official badge. Although boasting an all-black tail, VS-21's nickname is the 'Fighting Redtails'! The five coloured chevrons on the rudder of this aircraft have been CVW-5's CAG marking since its formation as Attack Carrier Air Group Five in 1943

▲ 'Beefsteak 710' (BuNo 159409) easily took the prize for the scruffiest looking S-3 aboard CV 63, but then it did have a head start over the remaining Vikings within CVW-5. The aircraft had already completed a 90-day stint in the Persian Gulf with VS-29 (it can be seen earlier in this chapter as 'Dragonfire 705') aboard CVN 70 when it was 'cross-decked' to *Kitty Hawk* in early April as a replacement for BuNo 160131 (modex '703'). The latter jet had been left back at NAF Atsugi when the unit deployed following a landing accident at the base on 30 March.

'We pride ourselves on always being in the right place at the right time for the air wing "strikers". We have tried to avoid "our" aircraft having to tank from other assets out of Saudi Arabia, Bahrain or Kuwait. Organic navy ops has been our primary aim on this cruise, for the more external assets you bring into the equation, the more messed up the missions tend to become', explained VS-21's Lt Chuck 'Wagon' Raley

◄ The co-pilot of VS-21's 'Beefsteak 700' (BuNo 159413) relays to the pilot the instruction to 'keep the power up', as signalled to him by the hook-up crewman squatting just forward of the nose gear of the jet. By doing this, the launch bar will travel up and over the cat shuttle, before falling into place in the 'notch' built into the shuttle itself. Aside from carrying colourful CAG markings, this jet also features a suitably-adorned refuelling pod – most stores of this type within the S-3 community carry the logo of American petroleum companies. CVW-5's boss, Capt Rick McHarg, was very pleased with VS-21's efforts during *WestPac '99*;

'We have regularly used the S-3s as the sole means of support for packages tasked with heading into Iraq on OSW missions. The unit has fully embraced this role when we have undertaken an all-navy "Vul" (period of Vulnerability) slot, and derived much pride from its ability to provide exclusive support. I would go as far as to say that this unit is currently the best S-3 outfit in the navy. They have had six elderly jets at full readiness on the "roof" throughout the deployment, attaining record levels of mission availability'

▼ This Viking is just a matter of seconds away from completing yet another OSW support mission. Lt Raley was one of a handful of S-3 pilots making his first *WestPac* cruise;

'There has been so much flying done on this deployment that I already have over 100 traps. Most guys would only get this amount towards the end of a six-month cruise – we have been on station for just eight weeks! On average, I have been flying two sorties a day. Typically, these will last between one-and-a-half to two hours, and whilst airborne, we will be exclusively supporting assets from the air wing. Although flying tanking sorties can get pretty old very quickly, it can also be rewarding when you are "passing gas" to aircraft on OSW missions. Getting guys in over the beach, and then getting them back to the ship, gives you a real sense of achievement. Should they have gotten into difficulties over Iraq, then it is our job to make sure that they have enough fuel to get back aboard the ship, and not have to recover to a land base, or ditch the aircraft'

◀ The two duty tankers are made ready for launching from the waist cats at the start of an OSW cycle. Although 'passing gas' on most mission, VS-21 did manage to complete other sea control taskings during CV 63's period on the line.

'About one-third of our missions to date have seen us operating exclusively as tankers. For the remainder, we have been carrying out SSC (Surface Sea Control), practice bombing and low-level flying. When performing SSC, we will establish a surface picture for the battle group whilst on station. This allows us to monitor the operations of vessels from other navies that may be operating in the same area. The Saudi navy is regularly seen sailing in our vicinity, as are French and British warships. Iranian vessels also infrequently venture out from their ports, as they like to have a look at what is going on – effectively exercising their rights to the freedom of navigation in the gulf', Lt Raley told me

ON THE DECK

▶ CVN 72's deck is given the all-clear for landing by one of the LSO's assistants (in this instance a pilot from VF-31), who nevertheless keeps a weather eye on the progress of the recently-recovered Hornet as it is marshalled towards 'Point'. Meanwhile, the LSO himself is talking to the pilot of the next aircraft in the recovery pattern through his radio hand-set, whilst another of his assistants stands behind him, pen poised to write down the landing grade for the trap in the LSO book. The CQ phase that CVW-14 conducted in September 1997 was the first chance for many 'nugget' pilots who had recently joined the air wing to impress seasoned LSOs with their 'ball flying' abilities. One such individual was E-2 pilot Lt(jg) Tom 'Heavy G' Gelker from VAW-113;

'This is my opportunity to show my more experienced squadron-mates what I am capable of. I need to put my best foot forward and prove to them that I am capable of learning all the intricacies associated with flying around the boat. I also need to show CAG and CAG "paddles", and anyone else who is watching the flightcam PLAT (Pilot Landing Aid Television) on the ship, that I can operate safely at sea'

◀ Each fixed-wing unit within an air wing will have a dedicated team of two or three LSOs, all of whom must have completed at least one operational tour prior to being given this crucially important job. One or two 'nugget' pilots will also be instructed in the LSO's 'art' as the deployment progresses, thus allowing them to become qualified in advance of their next sea tour. Wearing an appropriately decorated 'float coat', VFA-195's 'Paddles' seems happy with the line-up approach of this Hornet, 'in the groove' for a three-wire recovery back aboard CV 63

▲ As if denoting the danger of their job, ordnance handlers (or 'ordies') wear bright red 'float coats', jerseys and cranials. Working in teams, they are responsible for getting all manner of weaponry from the ship's magazines to the various aircraft parked on the flightdeck. Each unit will have its own dedicated team of 'ordies', who are fully trained in the art of loading/unloading and fusing the missiles or bombs unique to the aircraft of that particular squadron. This AIM-9M inert drill round (denoted by its blue body) has been wheeled out to an F/A-18C parked in the 'Crotch' area of the flightdeck aboard CVN 72. Up to four Sidewinders can be carried on this dedicated Aero-12C weapons skid

▶ Prior to the 'ordies' loading the AIM-9s onto the wingtip rails of the Hornet, the folded outer wing sections have to be cranked down by hand using a brace so that the round can be manually 'up-loaded'. Having removed the wing lock pins and laid them safely on the flightdeck, 'red-shirts' from VFA-115 get to work on 'Talon 214' (BuNo 163509) – although judging by the smile on the face of the brace operator, and the body language of his colleagues, the next launch cycle is still some time away!

► A new weapon making its operational debut during CVN 70's *WestPac* was the Raytheon AGM-154A Joint Stand-Off Weapon, or just simply 'JSOW'. Dubbed a 'smart truck' by users, it has been purchased by the navy to replace a variety of ordnance including the Mk 20 Rockeye and Mk 7 CBU-59/-99 cluster bomb dispensers, as well as the Walleye, AGM-123 Skipper and older GBU Paveway-series laser-guided bombs. The layout of the glide weapon is clearly visible from the elevated viewpoint, the nose section containing the guidance system, which consists of a combined GPS/INS unit. The mid-body 'strongback' portion of the JSOW carries both a set of high-aspect-ratio folding wings and the payload – 145 BLU-97 Combined Effect Munition warheads in the AGM-154A. Finally, the tail section incorporates the flight control system, which uses six moveable fins to achieve precision delivery against the designated target. Thanks to JSOW being a 'winged' weapon, the glide bomb can be launched up to 15 miles away from its point of impact if dropped from high level

▶ As with older ordnance, white deck gear like this Aero-12C skid is employed when moving a 1000-lb JSOW round from the magazine hoist to a waiting aircraft. Lt(jg) E W Osborn was VFA-94's Ordnance Officer on CVN 70, and here he describes how the various weaponry employed by the Hornet is loaded;

'Typically, a weapon is "staged" – placed into position beneath the wing or fuselage – and then the loading begins, along with a ritual chant. Amidst the grunts of heavy manual labour, the team leader bellows, "Ready Nose? Ready tail? Let's go. Bring it up! Straight into the hooks!" Once the weapon is latched in place, the "Ordies" let out a cheer, then move on to the next bomb.'

Although only C-model Hornets are presently cleared to drop this weapon, the results achieved by those units that have employed JSOW both in Iraq and in the Balkans have proven that it is the most accurate precision-guided munition in service with any air arm world-wide

▲ Bombs and missiles sit side-by-side to the right of CVN 70's island at flightdeck level. This area is regularly used to 'park' ordnance that has come up from the ship's magazine prior to it being uploaded onto aircraft scattered all over the deck. The green and grey LGBs are 500-lb GBU-12B/B Paveway IIs, whilst behind them are white Mk 7 dispensers full of CBU-99 bomblets. Finally, to the right of the LGBs are finless AGM-88 HARM rounds. All three types of ordnance was regularly seen beneath the wings of CVW-11's 36+ Hornets during CVN 70's *WestPac '98/99*

▲ VFA-113's Lt(jg) Lt Duncan 'Dingo' Clendenin was one of a number of 'nugget' pilots getting his first taste of sea time with a frontline unit aboard CVN 72 in September 1997. As his rather unusual call-sign revealed, he had spent his formative years growing up in Australia, his family moving to Melbourne when Clendenin was only an infant. Having completed his education to college level in Australia, he moved back to the USA when he decided to become an airline pilot. Clendenin soon realised that military flying would be more rewarding, and he duly obtained a degree in Mechanical Engineering through the Reserve Officer Training Course (ROTC), before selecting naval aviation as his chosen career path. He did well enough in his primary flying training at NAS Corpus Christi, Texas, to be selected for fast jets – he was one of only three from a class of 12 to be chosen, the remainder going to helicopters. Upon completion of his intermediate jet training on the T-2 at Meridian, Mississippi, and advanced training on the TA-4J in 1995, Clendenin was posted to the west coast Hornet FRS, VFA-125, at NAS Lemoore. He joined VFA-113 in March 1997, and during the unit's subsequent *WestPac* in 1998, Clendenin not only became a CVN 72 'centurion' (100 landings), but also achieved the best arrestment grades of any 'nugget' pilot on deployment

▲ Wearing a sand-coloured 'desert' flightsuit (popular with naval aviators 'going over the beach' post-*Desert Storm*) VFA-27's Lt Darrell 'Rimboy' Gregg gives the windscreen of the Hornet one final visual check before climbing into the cockpit and 'strapping on' his jet. He is wearing a standard lightweight helmet that has been customised with the gold and black mace insignia synonymous with his unit. Gregg was undertaking his second *WestPac* since joining the 'Royal Maces' fresh from the west coast FRS in late 1997, for he had participated in CVW-5's OSW deployment of the previous years aboard the *Independence*

▶ With upwards of 30 jet engines all singing away in unison prior to the commencement of a typical launch cycle, the only truly effective way for the pilot to communicate with his/her plane captain is through the use of hand signals. This 'brown-shirt' is instructing his pilot to ignite the right F402-GE-400 turbofan (NATOPS dictates that the right engine is always run up first) in his Hornet, which is parked in the 'Corral' area of CVN 70's flight-deck. Plane captains are amongst the few deck personnel assigned directly to the squadrons within the air wing, rather than to the ship's company

▶ Although the firemen of CV 63's crash rescue teams are used to high temperatures in their line of work, the 50°C ambient temperatures that they endured day in, day out, up of the flightdeck during *WestPac '99* stretched even their tolerance to heat. Each CV/CVN will have four or five specially-configured crash tractors which are strategically located along the flightdeck during launches and recoveries. Highly mobile, they are usually manned by three fire-fighters, clad in heavy asbestos suits. This rescue team has taken up a position in the 'Hummer Hole' during a recovery cycle, their tractor festooned with the 'tools of the trade'

◀ The diminutive figure of a female aircraft director motions the bulk of a fully fuelled and bombed-up F-14D forward onto waist cat four aboard CVN 70 in March 1999. The yellow-shirted director will remain in front of the jet until the hook-up crew have connected the aircraft to the catapult, imparting instructions to the pilot through various signals with her hands and arms. Once the green-shirts have confirmed that the jet is ready for launching, the director will hand the aircraft over to the catapult officer, or 'shooter'

SUPERCARRIER

▶ The most powerful warships ever built, the *Nimitz*-class nuclear-powered aircraft carriers are also the longest at 1092 ft, and the heaviest – CVN 71 and 73 weigh in at 97,574 tons when fully loaded, and the newer CVN 74 and 75 tip the scales at 99, 050 tons. The middle CVN in the second batch of three (out of an overall total of nine) improved *Nimitz*-class carriers commissioned into the fleet between 1986 and 1992, the USS *Abraham Lincoln* (CVN 72) is seen underway off the southern coast of California in September 1997. Compared with the other CV/CVNs featured in this chapter, CVN 72's myriad deck markings are clearly visible, denoting that the carrier had only just commenced air wing operations with CVW-14 following an extended period alongside. Indeed, the vessel had spent all of 1996 in Puget Sound Naval Shipyard in Bremerton, Washington, undergoing its first extended maintenance period since its commis-sioning into the fleet on 11 November 1989

▲ Slightly off to the left of the centreline and a little on the low side, should a pilot of a fixed-wing type be presented with this view during a landing attempt, he/she would no doubt be waved off by the LSO and told to make another approach. Despite CVW-14 having only been aboard a matter of days by the time I visited the carrier in mid-September 1997, the hectic tempo of the CQ period had already inflicted notice-able wear on the deck beneath the arrestor cables. Built over a five-year period in the Newport News Shipbuilding Yard in Virginia (11 of the navy's present fleet of 13 carriers have originated from here), CVN 72 has completed five *WestPacs* in just over a decade of service, and is scheduled to depart on its sixth from its home port of Everett, Washington, during the latter half of 2000

▶ CVW-14 joined 'the Legend', as CVN 72 is known to its crew, from the USS *Carl Vinson* (CVN 70) in the wake of *Lincoln's* 'YardPac' of 1996, the air wing swapping carriers with CVW-11. The latter had participated in CVN 72's first three *WestPacs*, undertaking myriad OSW patrols during these deployments, as well as operating over Somalia in 1993. With aircraft neatly spotted over the bow catapults and in the 'Corral', 'Hummer Hole', 'Patio', 'Junk Yard' and 'Finger' areas of the deck, *Lincoln* is ready for its next series of recoveries

▲ Two duty S-3 tankers are simultaneously 'shot off' bow cat two and waist cat three, thus signalling the start of yet another launch period from the weathered deck of USS *Carl Vinson* (CVN 70) in the northern Persian Gulf in early March 1999. Five Hornets can also be seen in various states of readiness for launching, with one jet already secured to waist cat four. The third of nine *Nimitz*-class carriers procured by the navy, CVN 70 was the last of the original trio of early-build vessels to be commissioned, entering service with the Pacific Fleet in March 1982. Named after famous Georgian Congressman Carl Vinson, who served in the US House of Representatives for over 50 years (1914 to 1965), this vessel was the first US warship to bear the name of a man who was still alive. Indeed, Senator Vinson witnessed the launching of the carrier in March 1980

▶ HS-6 SH-60F 'Indian 610' hovers over the bow of CVN 70 whilst a HARM-armed Prowler from VAQ-135 is connected to bow cat two, and a Tomcat and Hornet are configured for launching from the waist cats. During *WestPac '98/99 Vinson* set a new navy record for spending the longest sustained period 'on the line' since the end of the Vietnam War – 89 days. No stranger to these waters, CVN 70 has completed no less than seven *WestPacs* since 1983, embarking CVW-15, -14 and -11 during its 17 years of service to the fleet. Based at Bremerton, Washington, since January 1997, the carrier is presently in the middle of an 18-month overhaul period in the nearby Puget Sound Naval Shipyard, and is not scheduled to depart on its next *WestPac* until early 2001

▲ Lashed down between the waist cats, two plane guard SH-60Fs conduct simultaneous 'hot crew turnarounds' between launch cycles, swapping their three-person crew without shutting down the engines of either helicopter. As this view of I CVN 70 clearly shows, deck handlers will usually spot the deck so that similar aircraft types are 'chocked and chained' close to each other

▶ First off and last back. The recovery S-3 is well in the groove for landing on CVN 70, its successful arrestment marking the end of a 20+ aircraft mission into southern Iraq in support of OSW. CVW-11 flew 3405 combat hours during *WestPac '98/99*, this figure being the highest total ever amassed by an air wing assigned to OSW

◄ CVN 70's superstructure bears the traditional winged anchors emblem which symbolises the close bond that exists between the ship and its air wing. Immediately above it is the Flag bridge, which on *Vinson* in 1998-99 was manned by Commander, Carrier Group Three, Rear Admiral Alfred G Harms Jr, and his myriad staff. The navigation bridge is on the next level up, Capt David Crocker usually overseeing the running of 'his' ship from here during the *WestPac*. Behind the half-row of windows on the right-hand side of the island is Primary Flight Control ('Pri-Fly'), this vantage point being used by the Air Boss, and his assistants, to keep a weather eye on the activities taking place on the flightdeck. The island is festooned with various antennas, drum-shaped Mk 91 Sea Sparrow SAM illuminators being mounted on the starboard side of the structure and satellite communication equipment in the white-domed housings above 'Pri-Fly'. Between the two of them is the large revolving SPS-48E air search radar, and above this to the left is the antenna for the SPS-67 surface search system. On the top crossbar of the mast are two OE-82 'satcomm' receivers, with an antenna for the SPQ-9B fire-control radar mounted in between them

► The USS *Kitty Hawk* (CV 63) turns out of the hot easterly wind after completing its recovery cycle in the northern Persian Gulf in June 1999. Although upwards of 20 aircraft have just returned from an OSW patrol, and are yet to be respotted in the correct positions (note the two Tomcats, a Prowler and a Viking temporarily parked in the 'Street'), the 'ordies' have already got to work unloading unexpended bombs and missiles. These will be manhandled onto white gear and carefully wheeled back to the magazine lift aft of the island, or temporarily stored at deck level on the starboard side of the superstructure

► With a strike mission launched and well on its way into 'the box', CV 63's flightdeck looks almost deserted. *Kitty Hawk* is presently the oldest active ship in the US Navy, the carrier assuming this mantle from the previous forward-deployed CV, *Independence*, when the latter vessel was decommissioned on 30 September 1998. Built by the New York Shipbuilding Corporation in Camden, New Jersey, as the name ship in a class of three conventionally-powered CVs, *Kitty Hawk* was commissioned on 29 April 1961. A veteran of six combat deployments to Vietnam, CV 63 undertook its 19th *WestPac* in 1999. In that time, its decks have been home to CVW-11 (1963-76), CVW-15 (1977-81 and 1991-95), CVW-9 (1982-87) and now CVW-5. Homeported in Yokosuka, Japan, *Kitty Hawk* is expected to remain in service until 2010

▶ Two recovery S-3Bs from VS-21 are taxied forward towards bow cat one, the launching of these aircraft denoting that the navy package has gone 'feet wet' after completing its patrol in the southern no-fly zone. The Vikings will head north after leaving CV 63, setting themselves up in a refuelling pattern in order to provide much needed 'gas' to the 'strikers' (mostly Hornets) prior to them recovering aboard the ship. One of three conventionally-powered carriers still in service with the navy (along with *Constellation* and *John F Kennedy*), *Kitty Hawk* is just as capable as its more modern nuclear-powered brethren, and should remain at the 'tip of the spear' for a good ten years to come

APPENDIX

CVW-14 aircraft embarked aboard CVN 72 on 14 September 1997

VF-31 'Tomcatters'
F-14D Tomcat
164344/102
164600/104
159618/110
163902/111

VFA-115 'Eagles'
F/A-18C Hornet
163439/200
163440/201
163450/202
163456/204
163458/205
163470/206
163481/207
163495/211
163509/214

VFA-113 'Stingers'
F/A-18C Hornet
164640/300
164636/301
164648/302
164658/303
164638/304
164641/305
164634/306
164664/307
164682/310
164686/311
164220/312
164257/314

VFA-25 'Fist of the Fleet'
F/A-18C Hornet
164633/400
164639/403
164645/405
164654/406
164660/407
164676/410
164681/411
164262/412

VAW-113 'Black Hawks'
E-2C Group II Hawkeye
164111/600
164355/602
164492/603

HS-4 'Black Knights'
SH-60F and HH-60H Seahawk
164449/612
164072/613
164456/614
165114/615 (H)
165256/616 (H)

VAQ-139 'Cougars'
EA-6B Prowler
163888/620
163886/622
163520/624

VS-35 'Blue Wolves'
S-3B Viking
159745/700
159763/702
160582/703
159729/705
160576/706
160578/707

VQ-5 'Sea Shadows'
Det Bravo
ES-3A Shadow
158862/722

CVW-11 aircraft embarked aboard CVN 70 on 8 March 1999

VF-213 'Black Lions'
F-14D Tomcat
159628/000
163348/100
163893/101
164602/102
163899/103
164341/104
164603/105
159619/106
163903/107
163347/110
161159/111

VFA-97 'Warhawks'
F/A-18A Hornet
162835/200
162897/201
163098/202
163143/203
163100/204
163175/205
162860/206
163092/207
163106/210
163144/211
163122/212
163138/214
163107/215

VFA-22 'Fighting Redcocks'
F/A-18C Hornet
164060/300
164034/301
164036/302
164018/303
163990/304
164054/305
164057/306
164020/307
163992/310
164033/311
164039/312
164012/314

VFA-94 'Mighty Shrikes'
F/A-18C Hornet
164066/400
164052/401
163998/402
163988/403
164067/404
164055/405
163993/406

164050/407
164048/410
164027/411
164042/412
164021/413

VAQ-135 'Black Ravens'
EA-6B Prowler
163527/500
163528/501
163889/502
158816/503
161775/504 (from VAQ-209)

VAW-117 'Wallbangers'
E-2C Group II Hawkeye
164483/600
164488/601
164494/602
164108/603

HS-6 'Indians'
SH-60F and HH-60H Seahawk
164083/610
164079/611
164619/612
164444/613
165113/614 (H)
163792/615 (H)
165122/616 (H)

VS-29 'Screaming Dragonfires'
S-3B Viking
159387/700
160596/701
160572/702
159731/703
158871/704
159409/705
160159/706
159399/707

VQ-5 'Sea Shadows'
Det Bravo
ES-3A Shadow
158862/722
159415/723

VRC-30 'Providers' Det Two
C-2A Greyhound
162150/31
162171/37

CVW-5 aircraft embarked aboard CV 63 on 26 June 1999

VF-154 'Black Knights'
F-14A Tomcat
161621/100
161280/102
161293/103
162592/105
162697/106
161617/110
162610/111
162601/112
162611/113

VFA-27 'Royal Maces'
F/A-18C Hornet
164045/200
164025/201
164002/202
164010/203
164041/204
163996/205
164059/206
164016/207
164003/210
164023/212
164062/214

VFA-192 'World Famous
Golden Dragons'
F/A-18C Hornet
164899/300
164905/301
164909/303
164954/304
164971/305
164958/306
164962/307
164966/310
164969/311
164973/312
164979/314

VFA-195 'Dambusters'
F/A-18C Hornet
164968/400
164970/401
164972/402
164977/403
164980/404
164974/405
164960/406
164964/407
164900/410
164904/411
164908/413

VAQ-136 'Gauntlets'
EA-6B Prowler
163890/500
161242/501
158039/502
163529/503
163891/504

VAW-115 'Sentinels'
E-2C Group II Hawkeye
165295/600
165294/601
164107/602
163698/603

HS-14 'Chargers'
SH-60F and HH-60H
Seahawk
164797/610
164617/611
164459/612
164798/613
164460/614
164841/616 (H)
164842/617 (H)

VS-21 'Fighting Redtails'
S-3B Viking
159413/700
160604/701
160133/702
160584/704
160136/705
160139/706
158863/707
159409/710

VRC-30 'Providers' Det 5
C-2A Greyhound
162147/430
162164/431